The Language of Faith

Benita,

Speak

Faith!

M

The Language of Faith
ISBN 978-1-939570-02-4
Copyright © 2005, 2014 by Mike Keyes, Sr.
P.O. Box 91916
Tucson, Arizona 85752-1916

Published by Word & Spirit Publishing
P.O. Box 701403
Tulsa, OK 74170

Printed in the United States of America.

The Language of Faith

by
Rev. Mike Keyes, Sr.

Listen, for I will speak of excellent things, and from the opening of my lips [will come] right things; for my mouth will speak truth; wickedness [is] an abomination to my lips. All the words of my mouth [are] with righteousness; nothing crooked or perverse [is] in them. They [are] all plain to him who understands, and right to those who find knowledge.

—PROVERBS 8:6-9

CONTENTS

Foreword

Mike Keyes has been a longtime friend and co-laborer in the Gospel. Over the years, Mike has brought a number of outstanding messages to our congregation in California. One of the very best was his message on the *Language of Faith*. I was extremely pleased when Mike turned that message into a book. I believe you will be informed, encouraged, and inspired as you read it. Without reservation, I recommend this book to any and all believers that wish to grow in their understanding of faith and how it works.

Speaking the language,

Pastor Bayless Conley
Cottonwood Church
Cypress, CA

Preface

But without faith it is impossible to please Him.
—HEBREWS 11:6

For more than 20 years now, I've loved my study from the Word of God on the subject of faith. It is without doubt one of my most favorite subjects in all the Bible. I've studied it, listened to others minister about it on CDs, on the Internet, and in services worldwide, read many books and pamphlets on it, and with the help of the Holy Spirit, I have done my best to live it each day.

In several places throughout the Bible, God tells us that the just shall live by faith, so not only have I endeavored to live it from the day I got saved, I pledge to God I'll do my best to live it for the rest of my life. I want to please Him because I love Him. And if I'm to be pleasing to Him, I must learn how to walk by faith and not by sight.

God didn't say it would be hard to please Him without faith; He said it would be *impossible*. That's very strong language indeed. Not difficult, but impossible! No way! Nada! Zip! Can't happen! God is a faith-being, and He made us in His image and likeness. That means we're to be faith-beings like He is and use faith the way He does. Live by faith the way He does. Understand faith the way He wants us to.

So when we begin our study on faith, we quickly realize that there are so many things to know, so many directions of study we could take. For myself, even after devoting much time to the study of faith over these past 20-plus years, I know so little on the subject. Yet, I'm encouraged as well because I have, with the help of the Holy Spirit, managed to learn some things! I have learned enough to see faith take me around the world, start and run our ministry, protect me from harm, injury, and disease, pay my bills, and . . . you get the point!

But when you study on faith, where do you begin? God knows there have been hundreds, if not thousands, of books written on the subject. Untold numbers of sermons have been given on faith. So why this book? Why me? Why now? Good questions! I myself am not entirely sure of why this assignment has been given to me, but I do know that given the present set of situations and circumstances around us in the world today, faith is definitely something we need to hear *more* about, not less.

So how can I help? What can I say that hasn't already been said? Well, maybe it has to do not so much with my knowledge of how we live by faith, but rather with where I've been living by faith since 1980—the year I began my missionary work in the Philippines. Perhaps because I've spent most of my ministry time since 1980 in a country where English is not the primary language spoken. A place where I'm constantly surrounded with people who speak a different language than I do, and where the importance of knowing and understanding different languages can mean the difference between success and failure in outreach.

Let's take a look at what I've come to call the "language of Faith." If Hebrews 11:6 tells us that it is impossible to please God without faith, and faith is in fact a language (which I believe it is), we could say that it is impossible to please God without learning how to speak the language He speaks!

Lastly, as you read through my book, you'll notice the word "faith" is sometimes capitalized and at other times it isn't. Whenever we're talking about the Faith language, the word is capitalized. When we're not, it isn't. I pray this book will help you understand, learn, use, and become fluent in the language of Faith. Let's get started!

PART ONE

Understanding Faith As a Language

To be strong in faith, you must understand that Faith is a language as much as any language you may know. It has structure like any language and has rules that govern its expression. Let's find out about the Language of Faith!

CHAPTER ONE

We're All Bilingual

Throughout my life, I have always greatly admired people who are bilingual or even multilingual. By that, I mean people who are able to jump from one language to another effortlessly; who are able to speak and think in more than one language. I think the main reason why I've always admired such people is because it has never been an easy thing for me. It would seem some people just have an inherent ability to pick up and learn new languages. Especially in places like Europe, it's not uncommon to find people able to speak two, three, or four languages. Not so with me! From the time I tried to learn French in high school summer school classes, to my struggles to pass my Spanish courses in college, to my ongoing attempt to learn different languages spoken in the Philippines, I've known this is not something that I'm naturally gifted in! If I'm going to learn another language, it will have to be with massive amounts of help and grace from God! It's just not something I can master easily by using my own intellectual abilities.

On the other hand, my son, who was born in the Philippines in 1987, can speak my wife's mother tongue, which is called Cebuano, much better than I can, and I've been working among this language group since 1980!

Sometimes I get so envious of him! And when I talk about being "envious," I'm not referring to an ungodly form of envy, but rather a deep-seated appreciation and admiration for his ability to learn another language as he has done.

And as for my wife, well, she can speak Cebuano fluently, and since marrying me, she's learned English too. Now she might not be at the university level when it comes to communicating in the English language, but she's definitely able to jump back and forth from Cebuano to English better than I can jump from English to Cebuano!

Getting back to my son for a moment, he once had a friend who was a Filipino living in Germany. At the tender age of 18, she could speak six languages! Imagine six! Oh, how I marvel at such people! Why? Because it's always been such a struggle for me to even learn one extra language—let alone six! About all I got out of two summers of French classes was knowing how to say *"oui"* (that means "yes" to all you folks out there who haven't mastered French like I have).

Then moving on to college, and forced to take more language classes as prerequisites before I could move into my major fields of study, I chose Spanish because I already knew how pitiful I was at learning French. And after two years of language classes and language lab, about all I remember from Spanish is *"No sé"* (which, in case you're wondering, means "I don't know")! Yep, I mastered that phrase real quick, right after the first class I think. So for the next two years, I practiced using that phrase over and over again. On tests, during oral class discussions, when being asked questions from Spanish-speaking people, etc. *"No sé!"* "I don't know!" And then the other catch-all word I managed to learn in Spanish class was *"pronto"* (as in "get me out of this class *pronto*—like right now!"). That was it! Two years of hard work and to this day I'm still very fluent in saying *"pronto"* and *"No se."* I'm so proud of myself! My parents' hard-earned tuition money at work!

All Men Speak Two Languages Simultaneously

Because of my own challenges in learning other languages besides English, I so admire people who can seamlessly move from English to Spanish, Spanish to English, German to French, French to Italian, etc. One day as I was talking to the Lord about it, and just thinking about how nice it would be to be able to speak my wife's language fluently, the Lord spoke up in my heart and shared something that has really helped me in my study of Faith.

I said something like this to the Lord, "Lord, I really marvel at those who are bilingual and can speak more than one language fluently." And He said, "Mike, you're bilingual too. You just don't know it!"

"Really?" I said. "Wow, that's news to me!" The Lord went on. He said, "That's right. Not only are you bilingual, but all men are bilingual. It's just that most don't know it."

Here's how *The American Heritage Dictionary* defines the word bilingual:

> bi•lin•gual (b -l ng gw l) adj. 1. a. Using or able to use two languages, especially with equal or nearly equal fluency. b. Using two languages in some proportion in order to facilitate learning by students who have a native proficiency in one language and are acquiring proficiency in the other: bilingual training; bilingual education. 2. Of, relating to, or expressed in two languages: a bilingual dictionary. bi•lin•gual n. A person who uses or is able to use two languages, especially with equal fluency.

Notice here that, in this definition, a bilingual person is one who can use two languages with "equal or nearly equal fluency." A "bilingual person" is then one who, according to this dictionary's definition, "uses or is able to use two languages, especially with equal fluency."

With that knowledge in mind, the Lord went on to tell me that all men, because we're spirits living in bodies, speak two languages simultaneously. We speak one language out of our heads and another language out of our spirits. We do it all the time. It's just that most men don't know they're doing it. I didn't, until the Lord explained it to me, and I had taught on faith for many years. Not only do we do it all the time, but we do it every time we speak. Not some of the time, but all of the time.

Know the Difference between Head and Heart Languages

What is the difference between a head language and a heart language? Languages of the head are those we learn with our intellect. They are the ones we grow up with, and which we use to live and communicate with here on earth with other men. Languages of the heart, however, are spiritual languages spoken between men and God. Most people don't know this, so, of course, they wouldn't be aware of the fact that they're speaking two languages at the same time. No matter what language we may be speaking out of our heads, at the same time we're speaking another language out of our hearts or spirits. The head languages are for this world—the five-physical-sense world—while the heart languages are for the spirit world where God resides.

Taking this one step further, in our five-physical-sense natural world, a person might be bilingual in the sense that they're able to speak more than one language out of their heads, but if they are, they're also multilingual in the sense they're also speaking other languages fluently out of their spirits, while having the ability to use more than one head language fluently as well.

Different Languages of the Heart

Here's something else the Lord showed me. Just like we have different languages spoken by men on the earth today, so we have different languages spoken by men out of their hearts to God. As an example, we have the language of Faith, which is the topic for this book. But we have other languages too. There is the language of Fear, the language of Doubt, the language of Unbelief, and the languages of Pessimism, Skepticism, and Sarcasm.

Then there's my favorite of all spiritual languages—the Empty language! This is a language of spoken words that carry no specific spiritual purpose. In Matthew 12:37, Jesus referred to this language when He talked about "idle words" being judged on the day of judgment. Idle words are spiritually empty. They carry no spiritual force whatsoever. They're just spoken and released out the mouth, but that's about it. They carry no power to effect change, either for the good or for the bad.

The Bible uses other descriptive phrases to talk about the Empty language. In several places we see the word "vain" used to describe the Empty language. In Ephesians 5:6, the Apostle Paul admonishes us to avoid men who speak to us with vain words. In 1 Timothy 1:6, Paul tells Timothy to watch out for false teachers who have veered away from sound doctrine by engaging in vain jangling. That phrase "vain jangling" comes from the Greek word *mataiologia,* which, according to *Strong's Exhaustive Concordance of the Bible,* means random babbling! In 1 Timothy 6:20 and 2 Timothy 2:16, Paul again cautions Timothy to avoid what he calls profane and vain babblings. In those two references, Paul uses the Greek word keno- phonia, which *Strong's* says means empty sounding and fruitless discussions! Titus 1:10 refers to vain talkers. Using a Greek word similar to the one which talks about "vain jangling" in 1 Timothy 1:6, here *mataiologos* is used, which means idle, senseless, and mischievous talk from a wran- gler. I see that as a description of one who loves to talk and talk just for the sake of provoking someone to argue over issues which aren't important to God!

And finally, when using the word "vain" to describe the Empty language, we find it used in 1 Peter 1:18, where Peter talks about the importance of renouncing all manner of vain conversation. In the Greek, the words used are *mataios* (empty and profitless) and *anastrophe.* Coupled together in context in this passage from 1 Peter, *Strong's* tells us that it means those people are being told to forsake a lifestyle of engaging in religious discussions which are ultimately empty, profitless, and pointless.

God's not done describing the Empty language. In Ephesians 5:4, Paul once again admonishes his sheep to avoid foolish talking and jesting. Using *Strong's* as our refer- ence point, "foolish talking" comes from the Greek word *morologia,* which means silly talk and buffoonery. The Greek word translated jesting in the same verse is *eutrapelia,* which means lewd, vulgar, and tasteless joke-telling. In the same verse, Paul goes on to say such verbal conversation is not proper for a born-again believer to engage in.

If I may paraphrase, God is telling us to stop speaking the Empty language and start speaking the Faith language instead! Unfortunately, Empty is probably the one language that most of humankind has learned to speak fluently! Satan has so programmed us through the world system, which he authored and oversees, that most of us speak Empty all day long and don't give it a second thought! This is not by accident. This is by demonic design.

Here's the main point I want you to grasp: no matter what spiritual language we may be talking about, it's important to know that they're being spoken all the time, every time we open our mouths! If you don't know this, you'll never be able to appreciate the importance of becoming fluent in Faith.

CHAPTER TWO

Faith Is a Language

Walking by faith and not by sight begins with the understanding that faith is not just a conviction. It's not just an affirmation. It's not just a "title deed" to something not yet realized. All those words would accurately describe what faith is all about to be sure, but that's not what I want you to understand here. Yes, faith is a firm conviction in the final authority of God's Word. Yes, faith is our affirmation that what God has said He will perform. Yes, faith is like a "title deed" to something God has promised, but which hasn't yet materialized. All of that is true, but faith is also a language! It's a language of the spirit, and a language that when spoken correctly will open up to us the windows of Heaven and connect us with a source of divine power the enemy has no answer for.

> *The Lord GOD has given Me the tongue of the learned, that I should know how to speak a word in season to him who is weary. He awakens me morning by morning, He awakens my ear to hear as the learned.*
>
> —ISAIAH 50:4

This is a great verse to confess and believe for in your life. I've confessed it over my own life many times through the years, and I encourage you to do the same. Why? Because of what we're believing God for as we make these statements. Notice what we're expecting as we confess Isaiah 50:4:

- We want God to give us the "tongue of the learned."
- We want God to give us ears to "hear as the learned."

We're talking about two things here. A "learned" tongue and a "learned" ear. The word translated "learned" in this verse means to be educated or to be instructed. The writer here is declaring that by faith in response to this declaration, God will develop within us the ability to speak and listen in an educated, instructed manner. In other words, we're to believe that God will teach us how to be an accomplished speaker and an accomplished listener. What better confession could we make when talking about mastering the language of Faith?

As with all languages, the success in using the language of Faith lies in our ability to speak it well and understand it well, when it's spoken to us or around us. Meaning to say, we master the ability to speak it and master the ability to listen to it being spoken.

If You Don't Understand the Language, You Can't Respond

If you don't understand the language, you can't respond when it's spoken or written to you. For example: If I say this to you: *"Ala ka buok nakasabot niining libro nga akong gisulat? Kon nakasabot mo, palihug ipataas inyong kamot."*

Did you raise your hand? Probably not! Why not? Because you don't speak Cebuano, the native language of my wife in the Philippines. But more than 21 million people, if they read what I just said above, would all have their hands in the air. Why? Because they understand the language I'm using, and you don't—unless you happen to be fluent or knowledgeable in Cebuano.

Here's what I said in English: "How many people reading this book understand what I'm saying? If you do, please raise your hand." The reason you probably didn't raise your hand is because you don't understand Cebuano. But others do because it's a language just like English. It has structure, and there is an order to how words are organized and used to convey thoughts.

If you don't understand Faith you won't understand when God is speaking it to you, or when others are speaking it to you or to others around you. This is why Jesus was constantly misunderstood by even His own disciples. Remember this passage:

> *Then the Jews surrounded Him and said to Him, "How long do You keep us in doubt? If You are the Christ, tell us plainly." Jesus answered them, "I told you, and you do not believe. . . ."*

—JOHN 10:24-25

What did they ask Jesus to do? To tell them plainly if He was their Messiah. What was His answer? "I told you already, and you didn't believe Me." Jesus had already told them He was their Messiah many times, with sermons, parables, and scripture studies. Yet they were still asking Him to tell them plainly if He's their Christ. They were told, but didn't believe, in part because they didn't understand the language He was speaking. I mean, if I'm telling you I'm the author of this book, but you don't read or write English, I could tell that to you all day long and you wouldn't know what in the world I'm saying about myself, would you?

That's why Jesus could tell them plainly He was their Savior and have them stand there wondering what He had just said. Here's another example of this:

> *Then He also said to the multitudes, "Whenever you see a cloud rising out of the west, immediately you say, 'A shower is coming'; and so it is. And when you see the south wind blow, you say, 'There will be hot weather'; and there is. Hypocrites! You can discern the face of the sky and of the earth, but how is it you do not discern this time?"*
>
> —LUKE 12:54-56

Why couldn't they discern the signs of their time? Because Jesus spoke Faith and they didn't. Simple as that. He's communicating in a language they have no knowledge of, so no matter what He says, they can't pick up on it.

First, We Must Learn to Hear

As an example, if I want to learn Cebuano, my wife's native tongue, I need to train myself to listen when people are speaking it. I need to develop an educated ear so that when people speak Cebuano, I comprehend what they're saying. Once, I was flying back to the Philippines from the United States, and I used Asiana Airlines for the trip. When we stopped in Korea to change planes and connect to our Manila flight, the boarding area was full of Filipinos. As I walked around and among these people, I could immediately tell which ones were from my part of the Philippines. Why? Because even though there are 88 different languages or dialects in the Philippines, my ear has become trained and educated to recognize the Cebuano language. Many of those Filipinos were speaking other tongues and dialects which I didn't understand. But the moment I got close enough to hear people speaking Cebuano, my attention perked up and I knew what part of the country they were from. Why was I able to do this? Because God has given me the ear of the "learned" when it comes to Cebuano. My ear is trained to listen and comprehend when that language is being spoken. In the same way, from the time I was old enough to comprehend with my intellect, my ear has been trained to understand when English is being spoken.

Once the ear has been trained and instructed, we can begin training the tongue to speak the language correctly. At present, this is where my struggle is centered with Cebuano, but I'm getting better day by day! If people speak it, most of the time I can follow what they're saying. But if you ask me to use their language to express the thought they just spoke forth, I would have a hard time doing it. Why? Because my tongue isn't yet trained well enough to master the speaking aspect of this particular language. I don't know how to think in this language; therefore, I don't know how to speak it very well. (But as I said, I am getting better.)

Just based upon my own experiences in working among people of other languages, I know you must first develop the educated ear before you can develop the educated tongue. I mean, if you can't understand it when it's being spoken to you, how can you really use it when you speak yourself? Therefore, to obtain the instructed ear and the instructed tongue, certain truths must be understood about the language of Faith, as they would need to be understood with any language, whether it be of the head or heart.

Five Basic Faith Truths

Because Faith is just as much a language as English, Spanish, German, Filipino, Russian, or any of the other languages among men, it must be mastered by understanding five basic truths which, when applied, guarantee success in the learning of the language:

1. Faith has rules that must be understood.

2. Faith must be practiced and used.

3. Faith allows exceptions to its own rules.

4. Faith has many dialects and accents.

5. Faith surrounds itself with fluent Faith.

Let's look at each of these truths one by one.

Truth 1: Faith Has Rules That Must Be Understood

Like any language, there must be a certain structure to the expression. By that I mean Faith, like any language, has rules that govern its usage. To become fluent in Faith, it will require a detailed, working knowledge of the rules that create structure to the language.

Let me give you an example, using English. When I was a boy growing up and going through elementary grade school, I was taught all the rules that govern the usage of English. In class, we were taught many rules about the proper usage of the English language. One rule I remember very well, and maybe you remember this one too. It's the rule that says "i" before "e," except after "c." Remember that one? I do. In part because, at the time, classroom discipline was a bit different than what it is today. Back when I was in grade school learning English, the teachers (who in my case were mostly Catholic nuns) would do interesting things to the students in an effort to "encourage" them to learn English well. Things such as taking a 12" ruler and cracking it over our knuckles if we didn't remember the rules! Ah, yes—grade school! What fond, pleasant memories I have for that time in my life!

So to save my knuckles for future use, I was diligent to learn the rules that govern the usage of the English language. That's why, as an example, you spell "receive" the way you do. Why? Because it's "i" before "e," except after "c." You don't spell "receive" by putting the "i" before the "e" because of the location of the letter "c" in the word.

Here's another example. When speaking English, you must place the subject of your sentence in front of the verb, followed by the direct object, indirect object, and all the other elements that make up a coherent sentence. Remember them? Articles. Conjunctions. Suffixes. Prefixes. Prepositional phrases. And the one I loved so much—dangling participles! Oh, yes, those wonderful dangling participles! I can remember having to draw sentence diagrams with many angled lines showing the subject, predicate, noun, verb, direct object, indirect object, adjective, adverb, conjunctions, etc., etc.—well, you get the point!

Then there were those luscious dangling participles! Hanging there just waiting to mess up my homework assignments! I never could master the correct placement for those things in my diagrams! (At this point in my life, I've successfully managed to block out all my unpleasant struggles in English class with regards to a dangling participle—but I do have occasional flashbacks when I pull out my golden oldies and listen to the 1966 song by Simon and Garfunkel, enti-tled "The Dangling Conversation." Go figure.)

But if you jump from speaking English to Spanish, you must put the verb in front of the noun, which is the oppo-site of what you must do for English. If you don't know this, you will forever be trying to communicate in Spanish using English rules, and the result will only be frustration for you and for those you're trying to communicate with. Most Filipino languages and dialects follow Spanish rules, not English rules. That's why, many times, my wife Ethel will mistakenly put the verb before the noun in her sentence when speaking English—because she was raised speaking a language that follows Spanish rules of sentence construc-tion, not English.

It's important to realize that all language, whether it be of the head or heart, operates according to rules that govern the choice of words, arranging of words, and sequencing of thoughts to accurately communicate our thoughts and feelings to those around us. I'm using English to write this book, and this book is comprised of many sentences and paragraphs all carefully put together in a logical and systematic way according to the rules that govern the English language (at least I hope my editors think so!).

I can't just throw words at you in some haphazard, disjointed, and disorganized fashion and hope you get my meaning! No, if I want you to comprehend what I'm trying to say, I must use the rules which you and I have learned concerning English. I must first choose my words, then organize them into sentences, and then group them into paragraphs. Only then will you, the reader, be able to fully understand what I'm trying to tell you, right?

What happens if I mix up the words I want to use to make a point with you? You won't be able to respond! And more importantly, when speaking Faith, God won't be able to respond because He expects us to learn, know, and use the rules which organize our thoughts and convictions of the heart.

Can you follow me if I write something like this?

Spiritual to understands but God languages, only all responds: He Faith one.

Now if you're on some TV game show, maybe they'll give you enough time to unravel the above statement so you can win some money. But in case they haven't asked you to be on their show yet, and you're a bit pressed for time, here is what I said, properly arranged according to the English language rules:

God understands all spiritual languages, but He only responds to one: Faith.

Now I'm sure you could've deciphered the mixed up wording given enough time, but the point should be well taken. If you don't know how to utilize the rules of the language, whether it be a language of the head or heart, those people you're trying to communicate with are going to have a very difficult time understanding you. And if they can't understand you, they won't be able to respond to you the way you'd like. Think about that!

And as funny as it looks and sounds when we mix up our words like I just did, imagine how God feels when we come to Him and try to use our "Faith," knowing practically nothing about how to organize our words according to the rules that govern Faith! Imagine how silly some of our Faith "declarations" must sound to God!

Refer to the Textbook for Help!

Ethel's language, which is called "Cebuano," is also hard (at least for me) to learn because there isn't any organized, structured textbook approach to the learning of the language. It's all learned by "ear," as we say. I can't go down to the local bookstore and buy books or language CDs that will show me how to speak Cebuano correctly. It's amazing that 21 million people speak this language, and yet from 1980 until now, I've only come across one study manual which was published to help people learn to understand and speak the language correctly. Only one, and certainly nothing that even resembles a formal academic textbook. There are some small pamphlets designed to help tourists get by if they're in Cebuano-speaking areas of the country, but nothing of any serious nature. And trust me—if you don't have materials that show you the rules that govern the language, learning it will be much more challenging to be sure. I speak from experience.

When it comes to speaking the spiritual language of Faith, however, understand that there is a comprehensive textbook out there which shows us exactly how to master the language. It's the Bible! It's our textbook from God, showing us everything we need to know about how to speak Faith fluently. But just like any textbook in school, it won't do you much good until you get in there and start to study. That's why Paul tells us in 2 Timothy 2:15 to study to show ourselves approved unto God. Use God's Word to study and master the rules of the language of Faith!

So to speak Faith, you must understand the rules that govern the language, and there are a good number of them. We'll get into more about what those rules are later in this book. But for now, recognize that Faith is no different than any other language. It has rules that must be learned and adhered to in order to speak it correctly.

Truth 2: Faith Must Be Practiced and Used

As with any language, Faith must be practiced. It must be used. It must be spoken as often as possible, because the more it is used, the better the user becomes in handling the language fluently. Like any language, it has to be learned through practice and usage, because the more we use it, the faster we'll become fluent in it.

When I was in high school, and then later in college, I had to take language courses as prerequisites before I could go on to my major areas of study. In high school, as I mentioned earlier, I took French. In college, I took Spanish. I stunk at both of them! In part, I stunk so badly because I never spoke either language outside of class. I never used them in any day-to-day, conversational situations. I never sat down and tried to engage people using either French or Spanish. I never took a trip to Paris, as an example, or went south of the border to hang with the Mexicans. I never spoke it conversationally; therefore, I never really learned it.

Oh, yes, I studied and memorized the words of the language from the textbooks, but I couldn't make the transition to the real world. Now I'm sure there's some kind of learning curve where all of a sudden things begin to "click" inside our brains, and we begin to really use the language well. But I never got to that point, and I think part of the reason why was because, like I say, I never spoke the language outside of whatever classes I took to learn it. That's a big mistake—if you're trying to learn another language!

If you want to learn Faith, you must speak it. Speak it to God. Speak it to others. Speak it to yourself. Speak it and keep speaking it. Get comfortable using it and get comfortable hearing it being spoken. The more you use it the more proficient you will become in expressing yourself in Faith. In the same way I would become very good at speaking Spanish, German, Cebuano, or any other language if I just kept at it by speaking it all day long (or trying to at least), Faith becomes as natural to speak as your mother tongue just because you're using it all the time.

I am using the English language to write this book. I'm using all the rules I learned as a boy to communicate successfully to you, the reader, using the language we both know—English. I've used English since the time I was old enough to talk. It's been the language I've used every day of my life, from my infancy until now. As a result, I don't have to think about how I'm going to use English. I just do it. Whether I'm speaking it verbally to you, or writing a book like this, I'm so comfortable with English that I don't even think about all the rules I'm using as I process my thoughts and express them. I know English! Why? Because it's the language I've used day in and day out for decades. Now I may have to stop and think about what I'm saying to you, or how I'm saying it, or why I'm saying it, but as far as using the language itself, for me it's a no-brainer! I know the rules, and so I can use this language effortlessly. My knuckles rejoice!

This is not true if I try to use Ethel's native, mother tongue! Oh, no! I can't just launch out into some flowing discussion with those who speak Cebuano fluently. I've got to think it through before I even attempt to use that language. Why? Because I haven't used it like I've used English! If I try to speak Cebuano, I've always got to stop and say to myself, "Now, how would I say this?" I know how I'd say it in English, but I'm not at that point with Cebuano. Because I haven't used that language day in and day out like I have English, I'm not thinking in Cebuano— I'm thinking in English. Therefore, I don't just work her language subconsciously. I have to plod along because it's not "second nature" to me yet.

That's the way it should be when speaking the language of Faith, but the problem with so many Christians is that they're not habitual in using the Faith language. Therefore, whenever they do try to speak it, it's not natural to them. It seems awkward and clumsy. They're very uncomfortable in trying to speak it because they speak it so infrequently. They've not developed the ability to think in the language of Faith because they haven't used it enough to reach that point in daily conversation. That should never be!

Of all people on earth, we Christians should be absolutely fluent in Faith. As believers (in theory anyway), speaking Faith should be as natural as breathing. Every day we continue to exist physically because we're doing a number of things unconsciously. Breathing air into our lungs and then exhaling it is one of them. No healthy person ever wakes up and says aloud, "What a wonderful day! I think I'll just keep breathing!" Of course not! We breathe because it's just something God made us to do in order to continue to live.

In the same way, a Christian should be speaking Faith as unconsciously as they breathe air into their lungs. God made us in His image and likeness, so talking Faith should be as "automatic" as anything the human body is programmed to do to function day in and day out. A Christian should be able to talk the language of Faith anytime, anywhere, under any set of circumstances, and not have to stop to think about what they're doing or wonder if what they're saying is correct. Just like when I use English, I don't stop after each sentence to analyze my statements to determine whether I expressed myself accurately or not! No, I just know I did because English is my mother tongue. If I try to speak Cebuano, however, I have to stop after almost every sentence to ask if what I said was spoken correctly and if those I spoke to understood what I said. I'd have to do the same thing if I tried to speak Spanish, German, Russian, or any other language that I don't speak fluently.

Truth 3: Faith Allows Exceptions to Its Own Rules

Do you know that English is one of the hardest languages to learn by those who didn't learn it as their mother tongue? Why? Because of all the exceptions to the rules! Oh, yes, that's absolutely true. Linguists will tell you that English is one of the most difficult languages to learn because not only do you have to learn all the rules, but also all the exceptions to the rules! Interesting, isn't it? All I can say is, "Thank God I learned English as my mother tongue!" I have enough of a challenge learning other languages as it is, the ones that don't have as many exceptions, so I'm fortunate that English is the one I learned by default from my youth.

Faith is no exception to this truth. As there are exceptions to all languages of the head, so there are exceptions to the rules that govern the language of Faith. But before you throw up your hands in exasperation, never forget that God is our Language Instructor, and if anyone knows we'll make mistakes as we learn Faith, it's Him! So relax and enjoy the learning process! Don't put yourself under such legalistic pressure that your sincere desire to live by faith becomes a nightmare of worry and concern over whether every "t" has been crossed and every "i" has been dotted. Our mistakes won't negate the power of Faith, so don't let those mistakes discourage you from continuing on the learning journey with God. God knows our hearts, and if our hearts are sincere with the effort to learn Faith, His mercy will always be there to cover the mistakes we make as we're learning. So when using Faith and learning the language, don't be upset with yourself if you make mistakes! Making mistakes is a part of learning any language, and Faith is no exception.

As an apostle with a strong teaching gift, understanding this is a major concern of mine because, over the years, I've heard many preach Faith in such a way as to leave the listeners with the impression that using Faith is a precise science that leaves no room for error of any kind. My experiences with God, and my study of the Word, have proven to me that this is not true.

Why do you think the Bible says God's mercy is new every morning? Because we need it every morning! And in what ways do we need His mercy every morning? There are too many ways to count, but one of them is right here, in the arena of using the language of Faith. God sees our hearts, my friend, and if He knows we're sincerely trying to learn His language, and we're diligent to do our best to use it according to the level of knowledge we have at any given point in time, His mercy will overlook all kinds of mistakes we may make as we step out and decide to walk by faith and not by sight.

Now, of course, as we grow and mature, God will expect us to walk in the light of what we've learned, and He won't be so inclined to wink at mistakes made when He knows we should know better. But on the other hand, don't put any undue pressure on yourself! If you're truly doing your best to learn, let the learning experience be filled with wonderment and joy! It's so much fun learning Faith when we know God is right there to honor our progress and protect us from our failures! That's the way it should be.

Many times, I've heard preachers condemn those who, for whatever reason, failed to use Faith properly and didn't get the promised results they had embraced from the Bible. That is the wrong spirit, and I don't believe that type of stance pleases our Heavenly Father. I tell people that if their efforts to speak Faith didn't produce, don't worry about it. Life is one long learning journey, and we shouldn't get all worked up if we stumble a few times along the way as we work at becoming fluent in Faith.

I've been at this myself since 1978, and still I'm learning and growing, growing and learning. We've had a lot of victories along the way, but we've had some disappointments and "faith failures" too. And like any good baseball player, my goal is to constantly improve my "batting average" so that the victories happen more and more and the defeats and disappointments happen less and less. That's the understanding we need to have if we're to remain dedicated to the learning of God's language over the course of our lifetimes.

If our faith has "failed," we should be smart enough to know it's not God or His Word that failed. Obviously, something on our end prevented the power of faith from working, so instead of beating people over the head with condemnation and criticism, I just encourage people to go to God and ask for an explanation. Don't you think He'll give you an explanation if you ask Him for one? Remember, He's for us, not against us!

If your faith has failed you, ask God to show you where the error was made or in what ways you caused faith to fail. Then when God explains the reasons to you, make the adjustments and move on, armed with greater knowledge, awareness and experience. It's that simple! Sometimes we make things that are simple so complicated, and we do that to our own hurt!

When I try to speak Cebuano, I make plenty of mistakes, even when trying to use simple sentences and express simple thoughts. But, thank God, I've got a warm and understanding staff that helps me whenever I make those mistakes. They'll come along and gently correct me and show me where I made my mistakes. They don't laugh at me (well—sometimes they do!) and ridicule me. No, they just work with me and show me how I was incorrectly using the language. So when I get corrected, I thank them and try to assimilate the information being given to me. I don't run off in a huff, all offended and vowing never to waste my time with this anymore! If I did that, I would never make any progress!

But that's exactly what many Christians do when they've experienced some setbacks in their learning of Faith. At the first sign of trouble or tragedy, they burn all their Faith books, throw away all their Faith CDs, leave the church, and start blabbing all over the Earth that the "faith message" doesn't work.

Ask for Help and Learn from Your Mistakes

I ride bicycles seriously as a recreational hobby, and the first thing any serious cyclist learns is that there are two kinds of cyclists: those that have fallen, and those that are going to! Of course, you develop your skills and, to the best of your ability, you try to avoid falling off your bike. But if cyclists quit riding just because they fell down, they'd never enjoy the sport again! No, to ride seriously like I do (in spite of my constant ministry travel, and the fact I'm well into my 60s now, I try to ride my bike between 40 and 60

miles per week), I have to accept the fact that I will fall—
it's part of the learning process and part of the ongoing
enjoyment of the sport. I can't be afraid of falling, and I
can't allow the possibility of falling to discourage me from
ever riding again after I've fallen.

And getting back to those who want to quit trying to
learn Faith just because they've experienced a faith failure
of some kind, I wonder if such people quit trying to walk
the first time they fell down as an infant? As they lay on the
ground, sprawled all over the sidewalk, they may have been
crying, and they may have been embarrassed, but what did
they do? They got up and started to walk again! How many
times does an infant fall as they're learning how to walk?
Hundreds of times, probably. But eventually they master
walking, and when they do, they can look back with fond
amusement over the times they struggled to put one foot in
front of the other. They now can walk and walk and walk—
and not even think about what they're doing! It has
become as natural to them as breathing! Then once
walking has been mastered, they move on to running and
jumping and leaping and many other expressions that
follow the discipline of walking. That's how it should be
with learning the Faith language.

So when you make a mistake, ask for help and learn
from your mistakes! When God talks to you directly, listen
to Him and make the adjustments. And if somebody comes
along who's more seasoned in this than you and tries to
point out some areas which need attention concerning
your usage of the language, thank God for them! Don't get
mad at them. Don't get defensive! Just learn and grow!
Proverbs 9:8-9 says that if you rebuke a wise man he will
thank you because he knows the correction is helping him
become wiser! In context here, as we work at learning
Faith, it means that a truly wise man will not feel threatened when corrected, whether it's God doing the correct-

ing directly or through one of His chosen vessels—like a pastor, a missionary, or a good friend in the Lord. Instead, he'll thank God that he has another chance to grow and perfect the usage of the language all that much more.

Remember this point, because many have quit when they failed to understand this truth about the language. Don't get into bondage over the learning process. Don't get so "worried" or "pressured" to do it right that you lose the joy of the learning process itself. This is supposed to be a joyful journey and an enjoyable experience. If anyone understands the process of learning, it's God! Above all, He knows we'll make plenty of mistakes in our usage of the language of Faith, but that's all right with Him. What He's looking for is the pure and positive attitude of the heart. He's more than ready to help us when we mess up and misapply the rules of the language. That's what His mercy is there for—it's new every morning (Lamentations 3:22-23)!

Again I ask—why are His mercies new every morning? Because we're always in the School of the Holy Spirit, and there aren't any vacations! Every day for the rest of our lives, when we wake up, class begins! Every day we should be learning Faith, using Faith, talking the Faith language. Understand this point: our lives are continuous learning experiences, so don't get all bent out of shape if mistakes are made in the endeavor to walk by faith and not by sight.

Like I said earlier, if you make mistakes, that's okay! Join the club! We've all made plenty of them, but the good news is that if God be for us, who can be against us (Romans 8:31)? He's not looking for ways to penalize us for mistakes made. Rather, He's looking for ways to reward us for the growth that comes from making the effort! Remember that, and it will free you to enjoy the learning process!

Truth 4: Faith Has Many Dialects and Accents

Remember when Peter was in the process of denying Jesus three times? During one of those denials, in Matthew 26:73, people were accusing him of being one of our Lord's closest disciples. How did they come to make this accusation? By his speech, or as we might say today, by his accent. People have accents, don't they? All you have to do is listen to people who live in other parts of the country or world, and you'll quickly see that not everybody speaks English like you do! Yet it's still one language, even though the accents are wide and varied.

Every time I'm down south for ministry, I'm intrigued and sometimes even amused at how those "good ole southern boys" pronounce their words! And then on top of the southern way they enunciate their words, we have the very localized terminology which they use so often and so well. That's another story in and of itself! Let's just say it this way: if I had a penny for every "y'all" I've heard over the years, while down amongst the good ole boys, I'd be a rich man today! Are they speaking English? Of course, but it's their brand of English, with an accent which is very much different from the accent used up north in Vermont, which is very much different from the accent used in Cleveland, Ohio, where I was born and raised, which is very different from how they speak English in places like England or Australia or New Zealand or Singapore. It's all one language—English, but localized, individualized, and personalized by the people, cultures, nationalities, and localities of the English-speaking world.

Faith is the same way. Depending upon who you are, where you live, and what kind of environment you were born and raised in, your declaration of Faith will have a definite "flavor" to it. That's okay. Don't be concerned about that. Don't try to "sound" just like everybody else when using the language of Faith. As an example, if you see and hear some TV preacher using Faith and declaring Faith in such a way that blesses and inspires you, that's fine, but remember that you're not him (or her), so when it comes time for you to speak Faith, relax and let you be you! God knows you anyway, so you might just as well learn to be yourself when using Faith, because you certainly can't dazzle Him with a bunch of Elizabethan English!

Don't you love those guys who sound like everybody else until it's time to pray a prayer in public? Ask them to pray over the food at some function somewhere, and suddenly you'd think you're listening to Charleton Heston in a Cecille B. DeMille movie! The tone changes. The pitch changes. The words change. No longer just common verbiage, but now, we're talking like we're interviewing with King James for a position on his translation committee! What a joke, but unfortunately, the only one really laughing is the devil! How stupid that must sound to God when people try to put on airs in His presence.

No! Understand that Faith has many dialects and accents, so just concentrate on being yourself, and be at peace with that. There's a story in the Old Testament which talks about this.

> *Now Jephthah gathered together all the men of Gilead and fought against Ephraim. And the men of Gilead defeated Ephraim, because they said, "You Gileadites are fugitives of Ephraim among the Ephraimites and among the Manassites."*
>
> *The Gileadites seized the fords of the Jordan before the Ephraimites arrived. And when any Ephraimite who escaped said, "Let me cross over," the men of Gilead would say to him, "Are you an Ephraimite?" If he said, "No,"*

then they would say to him, "Then say, 'Shibboleth'!"
And he would say, "Sibboleth," for he could not
pronounce it right. Then they would take him and kill
him at the fords of the Jordan. There fell at that time forty-
two thousand Ephraimites.

—JUDGES 12:4-6

Here was this guy trying to disguise himself and escape the edge of the sword. To find out if he was really one of them, the men of Gilead asked him to say something in their native, mother tongue, which any man of Gilead would know. When he mispronounced the word, they knew he was not one of them and was killed.

Unlike the unfortunate Ephraimite, the good news about Faith is that God isn't going to kill you just because you're using your own "accent," which happens to be different from the accents used by many of His other children. No! Remember, He's the one who made us as individual works of art—no two people are the same, so He's not going to penalize you for using a localized, national or cultural accent with your Faith. It's a big, big world out there, and there are billions of people living in it. Don't fall for the lie that your usage of Faith has to sound like somebody else's or theirs has to sound just like yours.

God already knows your heart, so He knows if you're truly sincere about learning Faith. So even if you do "mispronounce" a few words now and then when speaking Faith, or use an accent different than someone else's in the body of Christ, relax. Realize that with Faith, as with any language, there are many accents, dialects, and personal "alterations" which reveal our own uniqueness but can never negate the power of our Faith declaration!

Relax! Be yourself! God knows you already!

Truth 5: Faith Surrounds Itself with Fluent Faith

The fifth and final truth to remember is that to become a master at speaking Faith, you must surround yourself with those who speak it better than you. That starts with God Himself, because nobody speaks Faith as perfectly as He does. You want to fellowship with Him as often as possible, both through Bible study and times of prayer. You would want to have the "Mary mentality" rather than the "Martha mentality," as described in Luke 10:38-42. After all, if you want to learn Faith, sit at the feet of the One who speaks it perfectly—all the time, every time. That would be the wise way to practice this truth.

And then, in addition to time spent with God, you'd want to find people who the Bible refers to as people of "like precious faith" (2 Peter 1:1). Once you find them, hang with them. As much as you can. Make them your new best friends. Love all your old friends, of course, but when it comes to learning the language of Faith, you need to surround yourself with those who know how to speak it better than you. People who have more experience with using the language. People who have spoken Faith and seen the Lord respond according to the "exceedingly great and precious promises" He's placed in His Word.

Anyone who has learned a foreign language will tell you, if you really want to learn to speak another language well, you're going to have to surround yourself with those who speak that language. Going to language lab in school won't cut it. Reading the textbook about the language will help you understand the rules of the language, how to spell the words and what the words are that correlate to your mother tongue, but to speak it you have to hear it being spoken. You have to listen to people using the language all around you. There's no substitute for this. Without this the learning curve becomes very difficult. Why? Because to speak another language you have to learn to think in the new language. You have to let that language become as natural for you to speak as your mother tongue is. As Isaiah 50:4 says, you have to develop an educated, trained ear to hear and understand the language and then develop the instructed tongue to respond coherently and correctly.

What happens if we continue to surround ourselves with those who speak the languages of Fear, Doubt, Unbelief, and so forth? Their languages will hinder us from using ours, and our communication will become mixed and, therefore, ineffective.

> *And half of their children spoke the language of Ashdod, and could not speak the language of Judah, but spoke according to the language of one or the other people. So I contended with them and cursed them, struck some of them and pulled out their hair, and made them swear by God, saying, "You shall not give your daughters as wives to their sons, nor take their daughters for your sons or yourselves.*
>
> —NEHEMIAH 13:24-25

Now I'm not suggesting we do what Nehemiah did to those who had allowed their Jewish language to become polluted by the heathens they were living with. But, the point should be well taken here. If you desire to learn Faith fluently, you're going to have to leave all your "friends" behind who don't speak it like you. Failure to do this will only delay your learning progress to the proportionate degree you continue to hang with your unbelieving buddies.

Are we to be unfriendly with all our old friends who don't speak Faith? No, of course, you should love them and do your best to help them learn to speak Faith like you. However, if they resist for any reason, you need to move on.

Stick close with those who speak Faith better than you and dump any of your friends who don't want to go there. It's just that simple. Love 'em and dump 'em, I say!

What about those of you who are married? Good question. I'm glad you asked! If you're married you need to realize the importance of getting both parties on the same page when it comes to the language of Faith. Unlike friends that come and go, your mate is with you for life, so you can't just "dump 'em" like you can with your unbelieving friends. As one part of the marriage relationship, you owe it to yourself, your mate, and your children (if you have any still at home under your authority) to learn Faith as quickly as you can and help your mate do the same. If they resist for any reason, love them and be patient with them. Unlike with social friends, you can't just "dump 'em" and move on! Why? Because of the nature of the relationship. It's different.

If it's your spouse, you must stick it out until God does a work in their heart on this business of speaking the Faith language. Help them come to the place where they realize how much power can be produced in the spirit realm when they hook up with you and speak Faith as you do. We'll cover this more later in the book, but for now understand the importance of surrounding yourself with those who speak Faith.

Make It Automatic

When I speak English, I don't have to stop and think about what I'm going to say in terms of how the language is structured and put together. Of course, I should be slow to speak in terms of what I'm saying or when I say it or to whom I choose to say it or how I choose to word my thoughts. Yes, that's very important, and the Bible has much to say about that very issue. But in terms of using the English language itself, I don't have to give it a second thought. Why? Because it's been the language spoken around me all my life. From the time I was old enough to understand, assimilate, and then speak the language, I've always been around those who spoke English.

For those who grew up in a Spanish-speaking environment, the same is true for them. Speaking Spanish is as automatic as breathing because they were raised in a home where Spanish was the dialect spoken by those who surrounded them.

For my wife Ethel, she was raised in a home that spoke Cebuano, a language of the Philippines which, as I said, is spoken by some 21 million people. She has had to learn English, in part because of her calling in ministry and in part because that calling places her by my side as my wife. And to her credit she has done a wonderful job in learning how to speak my native tongue, but when it comes to speaking Cebuano, no one has to tell her how to do it. And unlike with English, she doesn't have to stop and think her sentences or thoughts through before she tries to express them.

It's the same for me if I try to speak Cebuano. I can't just jump from English to Cebuano. It doesn't just flow out of me like it does her. But I will tell you this—being around people speaking Cebuano has been the only way I've been able to learn what I've learned so far. Why? Because unlike many other languages out there, as I've said, Cebauno has no real textbook you can go to and study. Now, from time to time, someone comes along and puts together a small pamphlet designed to help foreign tourists speak basic Cebuano, but in terms of a bona fide language textbook designed to teach people how to understand, learn and then speak Cebuano—it doesn't exist. At least as far as I know. So, to learn it I have to surround myself with those speaking it. If I don't, I'll never progress. I'll never master the language.

With Faith, however, we do have a textbook. It's the Bible. And, if we learn the language from the Bible, then surround ourselves with people who speak it better than we do, we're going to learn the language a lot faster than if we tried doing it all by ourselves.

CHAPTER THREE

God Speaks Faith

> *By faith we understand that the worlds were framed by*
> *the word of God, so that the things which are seen were not*
> *made of things which are visible.*

—HEBREWS 11:3

This verse in Hebrews contains a wealth of insight and information about what God has done in Creation and how He did it. This is one of those verses that has many messages within it. From one standpoint, we can look at this verse and declare that it's only by faith we can accept the truth that God created everything around us at some point in the past. This is true. But also, this verse simultaneously tells us that when God created everything as we see it today, He used His faith to do it.

The worlds (Greek word *aion,* which means the ages, and by implication, the planets, stars, and heavenly bodies out there in space) were framed. Or we could say it this way: God hung or placed or positioned the worlds throughout the universe just where it suited Him and pleased Him. Isn't it wonderful and awesome to know that every star you see in the nighttime sky has been positioned and placed exactly where God wanted it? Nothing is out there by chance, my friend.

How did He do this? With Faith. By using the language of Faith. How do we know this? Because of how the book of Genesis records the Creation in chapter 1. It says God spoke, said things about His creative intent, and what He said came to pass. He spoke His language of Faith, releasing the power within His own Word, to create everything you and I can see around us today.

He said, "Let there be light . . . ," and light came into existence (Genesis 1:3). He said, "Let there be—whatever . . . ," and whatever He said came into existence. He spoke! That's language, isn't it? Sure it is! God speaks Faith. It's His original language. It's the language of Heaven. He is its author. He invented the language. It's a part of His very essence and nature. It reveals His nature. He creates with it. The language of Faith is His language, and since we're made in His image and likeness, it should be our language also, just as natural to speak as English would be to anyone born and educated in the United States of America.

The Only Language God Speaks

Remember, I said that there are many kinds of heart languages, just like there are many head languages. Well, although God understands all languages, whether they be from the head or the heart, He only works with the Faith language. If we speak some other heart language, like Fear, He understands what we're saying, but He won't respond to it. He won't communicate using that language, because that language is contrary to His Divine Nature. The Bible says there is no fear in love and God is love (1 John 4:16-18). So Fear is not a language He speaks. He understands it, but He doesn't speak it. If you're using Fear when trying to communicate with God, He'll ignore you. He knows you're there, and that you've got problems, but until you start speaking Faith, He will just leave you to wallow in fear, doubt, and unbelief.

That's why it's so important to learn Faith, because it's the only language of Heaven, and it's the only language God speaks. If we don't learn His language, we can't communicate with Him and He with us. He won't talk to us until we talk Faith, and we won't understand Him when He speaks unless we understand Faith. Again, that's what Isaiah 50:4 is talking about—developing the instructed ear and the instructed tongue. Why? According to the verse, it's to give a word in season to him who is weary! I like that part of the verse especially, because it enables me to see the purpose in developing fluency in Faith.

Learning Faith is not all about me, but about me helping others. I'm not to learn Faith just so I can get all my needs met. It's not just about what the Faith language can produce to make my life more comfortable and plush. It's about taking me to a place where, by using this language fluently, I become a co-worker with Christ in reaching a lost, confused, and spiritually dead humanity out there. I have the means to keep Heaven's supply line open, while walking in the anointing necessary to accurately represent the risen Christ, who is the same Jesus we see in the four Gospels. He's the same yesterday, today, and tomorrow (Hebrews 13:8), so we need to show that to the world. How? One of the best ways is by tapping into what the Faith language can do. To have our needs met? Yes, but more importantly, for us to help others. It's all about outreach, my friend. That's what is important to God, so that's what He wants us to know about why the learning of the language is so important.

Learning to speak Faith puts us in a position where God can work His Word in our lives the way He wants to. We see this with examples from both the Old and New Testaments.

We especially see it in the ministry of Jesus. Men and women who spoke Faith were able to cooperate with God, hook up with God, get blessed by God, receive protection from God, and basically show the world an accurate picture of what God is all about.

So, suffice it to say that when we want to communicate with God, it's going to have to be by Faith. Not Fear, Doubt, Anger, Impatience, or any of the other languages of the heart. If we have a desire to make a difference in our world, and in our areas of assignment and influence, it must be through the Faith language. There is simply no other way, because as we have already mentioned, without faith it's impossible to please God! Impossible!

CHAPTER FOUR

People Speaking Faith

In the Old Testament, we have a great example of someone speaking the Faith language in 2 Kings, chapter 4. In the story, beginning in verse 8, we see a Shunammite woman and her husband build a prophet's chamber on the side of their house. The prophet Elisha would come through town periodically, so, as a gesture of love and support, this couple built an upper room onto their house so he would have a place to stay whenever he needed it.

In verse 13, in response to this act of kindness, Elisha, through his servant, Gehazi, asked the woman if there was anything he could do for her. After making a few proposals, the prophet found out that the woman, who was elderly, was barren and had always wanted a son. So the man of God calls her in and tells her that at about the same time one year from now she will embrace her own baby boy. At first the woman thought he was joking, but one year later, sure enough, she was holding her newborn baby boy in her arms.

But this is where the story gets really interesting. In 2 Kings 4:18, we see that the child has grown considerably. Exactly how old he is at this point we don't know, but it's

THE LANGUAGE OF FAITH

obvious he's not an infant anymore because the Bible says he's out in the fields with his father and their workers. While out in the fields he develops some kind of problem with his head, and after complaining about the pain to his father, is carried back to the house and to his mother.

> *When he had taken him and brought him to his mother, he sat on her knees till noon, and then died.*
>
> —2 KINGS 4:20

This verse tells us the child dies in his mother's arms around lunchtime. Notice what the mother does next.

> *And she went up and laid him on the bed of the man of God, shut the door upon him, and went out. Then she called to her husband, and said, "Please send me one of the young men and one of the donkeys, that I may run to the man of God and come back." So he said, "Why are you going to him today? It is neither the New Moon nor the Sabbath." And she said, "It is well."*
>
> —2 KINGS 4:21-23

Notice that when her child dies in her arms, she immediately carries him up to the prophet's bed, lays him down, shuts the door and goes to her husband. When she approaches him, she asks for donkey and driver to take her to the man of God. The husband, totally unaware of what has happened to their son, asks why she wants to go unexpectedly to him. The answer: It is well! Or, if I may paraphrase, she says to her husband: "Don't worry. Nothing's wrong! Just let me go and I'll explain later!" What is she doing? She's speaking the language of Faith to her husband! Does he understand it? Apparently not!

Then she saddled a donkey, and said to her servant, "Drive, and go forward; do not slacken the pace for me unless I tell you."

—2 KINGS 4:24

Does she say anything about the death of her son to the donkey driver? No. All she says is to hurry up and get her to the man of God as quickly as possible. So as the story continues, we see the woman coming up on the man of God, and as she approaches, he recognizes her. He remarks about it to his servant Gehazi and tells him to go meet her and see how she's been doing.

"Please run now to meet her, and say to her, 'Is it well with you? Is it well with your husband? Is it well with the child?'" And she answered, "It is well."

—2 KINGS 4:26

Oh, praise God! Listen to the answer when she's asked how everything is coming along back home! How's your husband? Fine! How's the business? Fine! How's your boy? Fine! It is well! Everything's okay! According to her, her marriage is okay, her businesses are okay, and yes—her child is okay as well. But wait a minute! Everything is not okay, is it? Her boy is lying dead upon the prophet's bed at the same time she's telling Gehazi everything is fine with the boy!

What's happening? Is she telling lies? Many would say that she is. No, she's speaking God's language of the heart—the language of Faith! Notice that at this point, neither her husband nor the donkey driver have understood the language she's speaking. And when she uses the Faith language with Gehazi and Elisha, initially they don't understand either. But because Elisha has a trained ear to the Faith language, he senses something is wrong from inside his spirit.

> *Now when she came to the man of God at the hill, she caught him by the feet, but Gehazi came near to push her away. But the man of God said, "Let her alone; for her soul is in deep distress, and the LORD has hidden it from me, and has not told me."*
>
> —2 KINGS 4:27

As she speaks Faith to Elisha, at first he doesn't make the connection with her. But after being caught by the feet (which will get your attention that something might be amiss!), he begins to realize: *she's trying to tell him something without telling him something!* This is how the language is handled. She goes on, as she's hanging onto his feet.

> *So she said, "Did I ask a son of my lord? Did I not say, 'Do not deceive me'?"*
>
> —2 KINGS 4:28

That's all he needed to hear! Now he understands what she's saying without her having to say outright that the boy has actually died. She and he are now on the same page. They're both talking the same language. They're both talking Faith. With an educated tongue, she's speaking Faith, and with an educated ear, he's able to understand what's being said.

> *Then he said to Gehazi, "Get yourself ready, and take my staff in your hand, and be on your way. If you meet anyone, do not greet him; and if anyone greets you, do not answer him; but lay my staff on the face of the child." And the mother of the child said, "As the LORD lives, and as*

your soul lives, I will not leave you." So he arose and followed her.

—2 KINGS 4:29-30

The instructions are now given. Elisha is now speaking Faith to his servant and tells him to go place his staff on the boy and to not waste any time about it either. Get there right away and do it. As Gehazi goes away on his assignment, the mother says that she's not leaving until Elisha personally comes to minister to her dead boy. So now we have the servant arriving at the dead boy first, with the prophet and the boy's mother in hot pursuit.

> *Now Gehazi went on ahead of them, and laid the staff on the face of the child; but there was neither voice nor hearing. Therefore he went back to meet him, and told him, saying, "The child has not awakened." When Elisha came into the house, there was the child, lying dead on his bed. He went in therefore, shut the door behind the two of them, and prayed to the LORD. And he went up and lay on the child, and put his mouth on his mouth, his eyes on his eyes, and his hands on his hands; and he stretched himself out on the child, and the flesh of the child became warm. He returned and walked back and forth in the house, and again went up and stretched himself out on him; then the child sneezed seven times, and the child opened his eyes.*

—2 KINGS 4:31-35

First the assistant's efforts to revive the child fail, then once the prophet gets there, he begins his ministry to bring the child back to life. He climbs on top of the dead body, stretches himself out on the boy, lips to lips, eyes to eyes, hands to hands. The body gets warm! He goes downstairs, walks around for awhile, goes back upstairs, gets back on top of the body now warm, and the boy sneezes seven times and wakes up!

And he called Gehazi and said, "Call this Shunammite woman." So he called her. And when she came in to him, he said, "Pick up your son." So she went in, fell at his feet, and bowed to the ground; then she picked up her son and went out.

—2 KINGS 4:36-37

What a story! And, what an example of how one woman used the Faith language to communicate her need to the man of God. If you read the story in its entirety, not one time does the woman openly acknowledge that her son has died. She doesn't say it to the boy's father, to her driver, to the prophet's assistant, or to the prophet himself. Instead, she speaks Faith, using rules that govern the usage of the language, and ultimately prevails because Faith always prevails!

And as far as we can tell in reading the story, the husband never knew his son had died. Neither did anyone working in the house or out in the fields. No one ever knew the boy had died except the mother, the prophet, and his assistant. This is how the Faith language is used. This is how it is spoken. As it says in Isaiah 50:4, this woman shows us how to speak Faith with an educated tongue, and the prophet Elisha shows us how to hear Faith being spoken with an educated ear. And that's all you need to protect God's anointing, secure His promise, and triumph over the devil at every turn.

Notice how she words her statements. First to her husband. She says, "It is well." Or, "No problem." Then when Gehazi asks her about how things are with her and her family, the answer is about her son. "It is well." Or, "He's fine." Then when speaking directly to the prophet, she says to him, "Didn't I tell you not to deceive me?" Or, "Remember what you told me about my boy being a miracle answer from the Lord?" And then even Gehazi gets into it, when, after putting Elisha's staff on the boy and seeing no results, he comes back and says, "The child has not awakened."

Notice how nobody using the Faith language ever mentions "death" or "dead boy" or grieves over the tragic death of the son. Not one time. Now, is that how most believers you know would handle similar circumstances in their lives? Hardly! And is that how you would respond if it was your child who had just died in your arms? Think about it. And someone might say, "Well, that's all well and good, but people nowadays need to stay in touch with reality!" To which I might say in reply, "What is reality?" What is "real" from God's perspective, not from the world's perspective? When learning to speak Faith, we must always remember there are two levels of truth. There is the truth of this physical, five-sense-controlled world, and then there is a higher truth, which governs the spirit world where God resides.

This mother didn't deny the death of her son. She didn't pretend it didn't happen. She didn't try to play mind games with herself, to convince herself the boy was really still alive. Instead, she simply chose to speak a language that addressed the higher truth that could govern the situation. God's power was available to raise the dead boy back to life, but only the language of Faith could be used to tap into that power. When Jesus said in Mark 9:23 that all things are possible to him who believes, He wasn't just whistling in the wind. He meant exactly what He said and showed us time and again that, when using the language of Faith, the user of the language can always tap into the truth that God's Word, when acted on and spoken in simple faith, can change any truth we may see down here in this world.

CHAPTER FIVE

Jesus Speaking Faith

When people are speaking Faith, the terminology used to describe real-life situations is many times quite different from what the "norm" would be. That's why, getting back to Isaiah 50:4, we must develop the instructed ear to hear what is actually being said, rather than just standing there scratching our heads because we don't understand where these "faith people" are coming from! Jesus is probably the best and most obvious example of a person speaking Faith. Let's look at a couple of examples from His life and ministry.

> *And behold, one of the rulers of the synagogue came, Jairus by name. And when he saw Him, he fell at His feet and begged Him earnestly, saying, "My little daughter lies at the point of death. Come and lay Your hands on her, that she may be healed, and she will live."*
>
> —MARK 5:22-23

A ruler of the synagogue comes to Jesus in a last ditch, desperate attempt to get the help he needs for his sick daughter. You have to realize that, for this man to even come to Jesus and openly and publicly request help the way he did, was a giant step of faith. This was not just anybody. This was one of the synagogue rulers. This was one of the

Jewish leaders of the day. This was a man who was part of a group of Jewish leaders who, for the most part, had rejected Jesus and His claims to be their Messiah.

Yet, here he is, coming in broad daylight to Jesus. Contrast that to the time Nicodemus came to Jesus by night, as told in John chapter 3. Why did Nicodemus visit Jesus at night? Because at that point he was still more concerned about maintaining synagogue membership! He didn't want to be seen with Jesus publicly, because he knew that it would get back to the Sanhedrin, and they'd be calling him on the carpet for it. So he secretly approached Jesus in the dark, so no one would know and possibly identify him as one of our Lord's disciples.

But Jairus was desperate, and desperate times call for desperate measures. Falling down at our Lord's feet publicly, pleading with Jesus for help before it's too late. If you read on for the next few verses, you can see that Jesus responded favorably to this prayer request and altered His travel schedule just to accommodate this man's need. So off they go to Jairus' house. Jesus, Jairus, and our Lord's entourage of disciples and followers.

While on the journey, beginning in verse 25 of Mark chapter 5 and reading down to verse 34, we see the journey interrupted by a woman who comes from behind, touches our Lord's garment, and immediately receives her miracle healing. Knowing within Himself that healing power has just left Him, Jesus turns around to inquire and find out who had done this. The woman, realizing that Jesus was looking for her, comes forward and tells Him her whole testimony. Meanwhile, Jairus is just standing there, waiting for the journey to resume to his house. Now if you're a parent who has children you love and cherish, I'm sure you can understand how difficult this must've been for Jairus. He knows his little girl is near death, and time is of the essence. I can just picture the scene in my mind, and the look of anxiety on Jairus' face, as he watches Jesus stop to minister to this woman now healed from the issue of blood.

But to his credit, he says nothing. He keeps his mouth shut. He patiently waits until Jesus is through ministering to the woman. Sometimes when using Faith, it's as important to know when to speak as when to keep your mouth shut! But nonetheless, just as Jesus finishes up with His ministry and exhortation to the woman, bad news arrives from Jairus' house.

> *While he was still speaking, some came from the ruler of the synagogue's house who said, "Your daughter is dead. Why trouble the Teacher any further?" As soon as Jesus heard the word that was spoken, He said to the ruler of the synagogue, "Do not be afraid; only believe."*
>
> —MARK 5:35-36

Now if you were the father of this little girl, imagine how devastating this news would be to you. He's tried his best to find and get Jesus to come with him, but now it's all for nothing. It's too late. His girl is dead! *No hope! None! Too late! If Jesus had just gotten there a little faster! Or, if only I had found Him a bit sooner. . . . Or, if only that woman hadn't come from behind, touched His garment, got healed, and delayed the journey!*

I can imagine all these thoughts are running through Jairus' mind as he hears those awful words, "Your daughter is dead!" But notice what Jesus says upon hearing the bad news. He doesn't acknowledge the death whatsoever. But rather, He turns to the heartbroken father and says, "Do not be afraid. Only believe." Wow—what an answer! It's Faith talking. It's the language of Faith being used to reestablish the excitement and anticipation of hope in God. With those six words, spoken in Faith, Jesus immediately confronts the situation and rises above the natural truth of the girl's death, to continue operating on the level that only the language of Faith can take you to. So the journey continues, but now Jesus leaves the crowds behind, knowing the situation requires a focusing in on the task at hand. He doesn't want any distractions with a noisy, selfish, shallow crowd. He wants only His closest and most trusted disciples with Him.

> *And He permitted no one to follow Him except Peter, James, and John, the brother of James. Then He came to the house of the ruler of the synagogue, and saw a tumult and those who wept and waited loudly. When He came in, He said to them, "Why make this commotion and weep? The child is not dead, but sleeping."*
>
> —MARK 5:37-39

Doesn't this sound a lot like the woman back in 2 Kings chapter 4 who refused to acknowledge the death of her young son? Jesus refuses to acknowledge the death of the child. Doesn't He know the child is dead? Of course He does—He was there when the bad news was delivered, and He was the One who encouraged the father to hang in there with his faith. So what's He doing here? Speaking Faith. Using the language of Faith. Calling those things that be not as though they are. Looking at the situation from God's perspective, not from man's.

Now if you were there that day, how would you have responded to this statement? Remember that Jesus is a total stranger to these people. There is no indication in the story that they knew who He was before He got there. Of course they knew Jairus and his servants, but who was this man that had come back with Jairus? Where did He and His disciples come from anyway?

Not only had they never seen Him before, they were totally blown away by this outlandish statement about the girl not being dead, but only sleeping! *Sleeping? Are you kidding? Are you blind or something? Is this some kind of sick joke you're playing on these grieving relatives?* That was how they received Him when He got there and made His declaration of faith. It wasn't pretty. It wasn't nice. It wasn't cordial. It was downright hostile.

> *And they ridiculed Him. But when He had put them all outside, He took the father and the mother of the child, and those who were with Him, and entered where the child was lying.*
>
> —MARK 5:40

Look at how the people at Jairus' house reacted when He came in and announced that the little 12-year-old girl was not dead—only sleeping! They ridiculed Him. Other translations say they laughed Him to scorn. This was not a happy kind of laughter. This was the deriding kind. The kind of laughter that denotes utter contempt for the one being laughed at. This is how they responded when Jesus spoke Faith at that funeral service that day.

What did He do when they laughed at Him? He put them all out. Remember what I said before—if your "friends" don't speak Faith, or if you find yourself surrounded by people who don't understand Faith like you do, you should do what Jesus did. Get rid of them. Tell them to leave. Politely (if that's possible) ask them to go away. Or you go away if you can. Whatever. Do what you must in order to surround yourself with people who speak Faith, or at least are people who are not going to actively try and discourage you from speaking Faith.

> *Then He took the child by the hand, and said to her, "Talitha, cumi," which is translated, "Little girl, I say to you, arise." Immediately the girl arose and walked, for she*

*was twelve years of age. And they were overcome with
great amazement.*

—MARK 5:41-42

We see Jesus using the language of Faith to raise a dead girl
back to life. Later, we see Him using the language again to
raise His good friend Lazarus from the dead also.

> *Now a certain man was sick, Lazarus of Bethany, the
> town of Mary and her sister Martha. It was that Mary
> who anointed the Lord with fragrant oil and wiped His
> feet with her hair, whose brother Lazarus was sick.
> Therefore the sisters sent to Him, saying, "Lord, behold, he
> whom You love is sick." When Jesus heard that, He said,
> "This sickness is not unto death, but for the glory of God,
> that the Son of God may be glorified through it."*
>
> *Now Jesus loved Martha and her sister and Lazarus.
> So, when He heard that he was sick, He stayed two more
> days in the place where He was. Then after this He said to
> the disciples, "Let us go to Judea again." The disciples said
> to Him, "Rabbi, lately the Jews sought to stone You, and
> are You going there again?"*
>
> *Jesus answered, "Are there not twelve hours in the day?
> If anyone walks in the day, he does not stumble, because he
> sees the light of this world. But if one walks in the night,
> he stumbles, because the light is not in him." These things
> He said, and after that He said to them, "Our friend
> Lazarus sleeps, but I go that I may wake him up."*
>
> *Then His disciples said, "Lord, if he sleeps he will get
> well." However, Jesus spoke of his death, but they thought
> that He was speaking about taking rest in sleep. Then
> Jesus said to them plainly, "Lazarus is dead. And I am
> glad for your sakes that I was not there, that you may
> believe. Nevertheless let us go to him." Then Thomas, who*

is called the Twin, said to his fellow disciples, "Let us also go, that we may die with Him."

—JOHN 11:1-16

This story is a carbon copy of the story we examined from Mark chapter 5. The only difference really is the person who was raised from the dead. In Mark's Gospel, it was a twelve-year-old girl that Jesus had never met before. In this story from John's Gospel, it's His good friend Lazarus. But the victory was wrought the same way—by using the language of Faith.

Notice that after Jesus was informed of Lazarus' condition, He purposely waited in the same place and didn't rush to the side of His sick friend. No, the Bible says He remained in the same place two days after being told Lazarus was sick and dying. Then, almost casually, He says to His disciples, "Let's go back to Judea!"

The disciples can't believe it! The Jews were just trying to kill Jesus in Judea, and now He wants to go back? I'm sure they're thinking, *What's wrong with Jesus? Does He have short-term memory loss or something?* But our Lord is actually on a mission and has begun declaring Faith to get the job done. God told Him to purposely wait until Lazarus had died, and now, He's being instructed to go raise him from the dead. Why? According to verse 15, it's so that all the bystanders will believe! Isn't God good? There's no sickness that can stand in the way of Faith, and death is certainly no problem either.

It's like what Jesus said to the crowd who heard Him tell the paralyzed man that his sins were forgiven (Mark 2:1-12). When Jesus told the man his sins were forgiven, the Jews began mumbling and murmuring against Him. How did He respond? He said, "What's easier for me to say? Your sins are forgiven, or take up your bed and walk?" In other words, He's telling His critics, "Okay, since you don't believe I have authority to do something you can't see, I'll use My authority to do something you can see." What did He do? He told the paralyzed man to rise, fold up his mat and walk home.

As far as God is concerned, there's no difference between a sick Lazarus and a dead Lazarus. Jesus had authority over both and proved it time and again during His earthly ministry. Healing Lazarus from his sickness was no problem for Jesus any more than raising him from the dead would be. And if God had told Jesus to rush right over and pray to heal Lazarus before he died, Jesus would've done so. But in God's wisdom, He knew it would help create more faith in the people if they saw Jesus raise Lazarus from the dead rather than just heal him from sickness. So, He had Jesus wait a few days until Lazarus had died, then sent the Lord to raise him up.

Notice carefully our Lord's terminology in this passage. Notice how He's using Faith to communicate with His disciples. When they questioned Him about the wisdom of going back to Judea, unaware of what He was being told by God to do there, He answered them with a question. He said, "Are there not twelve hours in the day? If anyone walks in the day, he does not stumble, because he sees the light of this world. But if one walks in the night, he stumbles, because the light is not in him." Does this sound a bit "off the wall" to you? It would to many, and it certainly did to His disciples. They obviously were not following His train of thought and didn't understand what He was saying. That's the way it is with Faith. When you speak it around people who don't have a trained ear to hear it, they're not going to be able to follow you. It will seem to them as if you're not making any sense with your speech.

But Jesus is speaking Faith, just like He did back in Mark chapter five when He raised the little 12-year-old back to life. They didn't understand His terminology then, and His disciples aren't understanding it now. And with each statement He makes relative to the passing of Lazarus, they become more and more confused and lost.

He goes on to say, "Our friend Lazarus sleeps, but I go that I may wake him up." Then His disciples answered and said, if I may paraphrase, "Lord, if he is only sleeping, why do we need to be bothered about it?" Then verse 13 shows us just how "out of it" His disciples were. It says that Jesus was speaking of his good friend's death but they didn't understand that. They thought He was talking about Lazarus taking a nap. Friends, it's obvious they don't have a clue as to what Jesus is talking about!

Like the family and friends attending the 12-year-old's wake in Mark chapter 5, it's obvious these disciples are not on the same page with Jesus. They're not communicating. He's talking, but they're not understanding. Why? Because once again, He's speaking Faith, and they're not understanding because they don't know how to speak that language. Realizing that His own team was clueless, Jesus finally lowers His conversation to their level of understanding and says plainly that Lazarus had died.

This sort of thing went on all through the ministry of Jesus. He was constantly saying things that seemed weird and unconnected to those He was speaking to. The reason for this was because He was speaking a language nobody else understood, including His own men. Take for example another episode where Jesus and His team have just crossed the lake and are disembarking on the other side. Jesus turns to them and says something they are completely unable to understand.

And He left them, and getting into the boat again, departed to the other side. Now the disciples had forgotten to take bread, and they did not have more than one loaf with them in the boat. Then He charged them, saying, "Take heed, beware of the leaven of the Pharisees and the leaven of Herod."

And they reasoned among themselves, saying, "It is because we have no bread."

But Jesus, being aware of it, said to them, "Why do you reason because you have no bread? Do you not yet perceive nor understand? Is your heart still hardened? Having eyes, do you not see? And having ears, do you not hear? And do you not remember? When I broke the five loaves for the five thousand, how many baskets full of fragments did you take up?"

They said to Him, "Twelve."

"Also, when I broke the seven for the four thousand, how many large baskets full of fragments did you take up?"

And they said, "Seven."

So He said to them, "How is it you do not understand?"

—MARK 8:13-21

He's trying to warn them about the false teachings of the Pharisees and Sadducees, but they think He's asking who brought the bread for lunch! I can just see Jesus standing there, rolling His eyes heavenward and wondering how long it's going to take for these guys to finally get it. You can almost hear the exasperation in His reply to them. As they're all looking at each other, trying to find out who dropped the ball and forgot to bring the bread, Jesus says, "Don't you guys understand yet? I'm not talking about bread, you clowns. I'm talking about the 'leaven' of the Pharisees—the false food they're feeding the Jews—misleading them and misguiding them concerning the scriptures."

Notice especially verse 18. He asks them questions in His exasperation with them. "You have eyes, but why can't you see? You have ears, but why can't you hear? Don't you remember how I fed thousands miraculously by the hand of God?" What is He trying to explain to them? That if it was an issue of food, He could just stand in faith, use His authority and create as much food as they needed. He had done it before on more than one occasion. Food was not the issue here—false teaching was, and He was trying to get them to understand that the food the Pharisees were offering the people was spiritual poison. He was trying to tell them to beware, stay away from it, and don't go near it.

It's interesting that as He's upbraiding them for their lack of understanding, He talks about their eyes and ears. Remember Isaiah 50:4, talking about the importance of having educated ears? Jesus is referring to that here. He wants His disciples to learn Faith, so that when He speaks it and tries to teach them something important, they'll be able to follow along and get the points He's trying to make.

I wonder how dumb you and I would be if we were in that boat and Jesus made the same statements to us about the false teachings of the Pharisees. I'd venture to say most of us would be as clueless as they were! More than once Jesus just plain got frustrated with His team because they were so slow in grasping the language of Faith. Remember this question He shouted out when His disciples failed to cast out one demon while He was away on the mountaintop?

> He answered him and said, "O faithless generation, how long shall I be with you? How long shall I bear with you? Bring him to Me."
>
> —MARK 9:19

"You faithless generation!" He was mad! He was upset, and He was frustrated with all of them! Not just with the father of the demon-possessed boy, but most especially with His own disciples. He cries out in frustration, "How long must I put up with you people?" That doesn't sound like He was very impressed with their ability to use Faith! According to Him, it was a "faithless" generation. They had no faith in their hearts towards God, and they had no knowledge of the Faith language. That sounds like so many in the body of Christ today!

Does it sound like you? I hope not!

CHAPTER SIX

Faith Connects Us with God's Power

Speaking Faith connects you with the power that is all around us every day. I'm reminded of something Jesus told Rev. Kenneth Hagin in one of his visions of the Lord. During the vision, Hagin said Jesus told him that power was present everywhere. The Lord was trying to show Rev. Hagin that all the power needed to change any situation, move any mountain, or overcome any challenge was already here. He's called the Holy Spirit! He's always here, ready to respond when words of Faith are spoken.

Remember in Genesis chapter 1, when the Spirit of the Lord was hovering over the face of the waters (Genesis 1:2)? When did He move to create everything we now see? When God spoke Faith words. Nothing happened until God spoke Faith. Until then the Holy Spirit was just "hovering," not "creating." But when God spoke and said, "Let there be light," the Holy Spirit took those words of Faith and used them to create everything we now see in this world.

Guess what? Nothing has changed! It still works the same way for today! Paul said that when we exercise the "spirit of faith," we believe and then we speak (2 Corinthians 4:13)!

And when we speak the language called Faith, the power of the Holy Spirit is right there to make good on our declarations. It's called the authority of the believer.

Jesus spoke Faith from the time Jairus approached Him to the moment He took the little dead girl by the hand and raised her from the dead. From the time He declared Lazarus' destiny to the time He called him out of the tomb. While His disciples argued over who forgot the bread! While the Jews murmured about His declaration that the paralyzed man's sins were forgiven.

No one else spoke it, but that didn't matter, and it shouldn't matter with you or me. Even if we can't find those around us at any given time who understand and speak Faith, it shouldn't deter us from using the language ourselves. It's enough to know God understands this language and delights in responding to it when spoken by men—by anyone, anywhere! He's no respecter of persons (Acts 10:34). With or without support from others, our motto should be like that of an old western TV series of the 1960s called "Paladin." The star of that show was a hired gun who always carried around a business card that said "Have Gun, Will Travel." Well, for us today, our motto should be along the same lines. Only ours will say "Have Faith, Will Speak!"

The Works He Did Are the Works We Can Do

Someone will always come along right about now and say, "But that was Jesus!" As if to imply we can't use Faith and get the same results like He did. But friends, Jesus Himself said we could, so if He says we can, then we can!

> *"Most assuredly, I say to you, he who believes in Me, the works that I do he will do also; and greater works than these he will do, because I go to my Father."*

> —JOHN 14:12

If you're a believer, He's talking about you in this verse. The works He did, you can do also. What works? The works of men speaking Faith. The works which both validate and enforce the covenant we have with God today. The works which set the captives free. Remember, Jesus was all man as well as all God, and this verse is not a reference to the works He accomplished on the cross as our sin substitute. No, no, no! This verse, if read in context, clearly indicates that the works He's talking about are the works done to confirm the message of the Gospel. This was His humanity in manifestation, not His deity.

You see, aside from coming down from Heaven and emptying Himself of all the privileges of deity (Philippians 2:5-8), I don't believe Jesus did one single thing on this earth as God. He did it all as a man. He had to! Otherwise, the devil could call the entire exercise unfair and invalid. No, the test had to be fair and square. A man had to live his entire life sin-free and successfully fulfill the Mosaic Law. A man was the one who caused the fall, and a man had to cause the redemption. That's why Adam is called the first Adam and Jesus is called the last Adam (1 Corinthians 15:45).

Remember Mark 16:15-18, which is what we call the "Great Commission"? Jesus tells us to go into all the world and preach the Gospel to every creature. What does He say after that?

> *"And these signs will follow those who believe: In My name they will cast out demons; they will speak with new tongues; they will take up serpents; and if they drink*

anything deadly, it will by no means hurt them; they will lay hands on the sick, and they will recover."

—MARK 16:17-18

If you're a believer, these signs should be following you as you proclaim the Gospel to those around you. What kinds of signs? Miracles, healings, and manifestations of the presence and power of the Holy Spirit. In other words, it's the "works" Jesus spoke about in John 14:12. These are the "works" we do in His Name, as we tap into the power all around us by speaking the language of Faith.

It's like how we tap into the power of electricity. Electric current is all around you. It's in the wires behind the wall. But just having all that power around you does you no good until you take an electric cord and insert the plug into the socket. When you do that, you've made the connection, and suddenly all that electric current is yours to use. That's the way it is with using Faith to make the connection with the power of God all around us.

Notice what happened when the disciples obeyed the Great Commission.

So then, after the Lord had spoken to them, He was received up into heaven, and sat down at the right hand of God. And they went out and preached everywhere, the Lord working with them and confirming the word through the accompanying signs. Amen.

—MARK 16:19-20

What was the Lord doing? He was confirming the word they were speaking. He was validating their message. He was proving, not by their message but by His power, that He was alive and the same yesterday, today, and forever. They were doing the works in His Name, exactly like He was doing the works in the Name of His Father God. He spoke

Faith, and God honored it with signs and wonders to confirm His message (see John 10:31-39 and John 14:9-14). In the same way, when we speak Faith in the Name of Jesus, He will honor it to confirm the Gospel we preach. He told them that they would be doing the works He did, and even greater works! He's telling us the same thing today!

What would be the greater works? I believe the greater works are leading men into Christ, what He called being "born again." Bringing them to the feet of Jesus and leading them through their decision to make Jesus Lord of their lives. Those are the greater works, because that's something Jesus didn't do while He was on earth. That was not His mission. His mission on Earth was to be the last prophet of the Old Covenant, fulfill the law, be our sin substitute, and legally bring us back to God through His death and resurrection.

Our job is now to go into the world and proclaim this and bring people to Christ. We're to help people speak the language of Faith when they hear the Word of God being preached (Romans 10:9-10). That's our job now. That's the greater work! Why does Jesus consider these to be the greater works? Because no miracle that changes the body can match the miracle that changes the human heart! The greatest miracle on earth has nothing to do with something done to a physical body, but rather, what's done on the inside of a man, when his spirit is actually recreated by the power of the Holy Spirit. That's the greater work! That's the greatest miracle on earth!

And how does this happen? When we speak Faith. By putting the Word of God in our mouths and proclaiming it wherever we go, just like Jesus did. Faith comes by hearing, and hearing by the Word of God (Romans 10:17). Well, if it comes by hearing, that means somebody is speaking it. Either you're speaking it aloud, or someone else is. A careful study of the subject of words and the creative power within them will help you understand that the language of Faith, like all languages, must be spoken to be used. Not thought, but spoken! To communicate I must speak! I must be heard! That's why I've always told people that if they want to grow in faith, they must discipline themselves to speak the Word of God that covers the circumstances they're trying to change with their Faith.

Jesus knew how to speak in Faith, not just think in Faith. In fact, when Joshua 1:8 tells us to meditate in the Law (God's Word) to achieve prosperity and success, the word "meditate" means to mutter or speak softly to yourself. Not think it, but say it—loud enough to hear yourself speaking. Every miracle Jesus performed involved Him speaking Faith, and it must be that way with you and me, too, when we minister in His Name.

Get Ready to Be Misunderstood and Maligned

Jesus was fluent in Faith. He spoke it everywhere He went, which as I said, explains to us why His messages, parables, teachings, illustrations, and answers were so perplexing to the people. Even His own disciples struggled with His teachings. How often would you see the disciples come up to Jesus privately after one of our Lord's Bible studies and ask Him for an explanation of what He had just taught the people?

If you go back and carefully read through the sermons He gave, as recorded in the four Gospels, you can easily see why His listeners were so confused all the time. Jesus was speaking a language no one understood, including His own disciples. Because He was speaking a language no one understood, He was constantly being misunderstood, misquoted, maligned, ridiculed, criticized, and laughed at. Get used to it, because the servant is not above his master (Matthew 10:24-25)!

If they did it with Jesus, and you use Faith like He did, they'll be doing it to you! When you speak Faith, you're going to get the same type of response Jesus got when He spoke it. You'll be laughed at. Made fun of. Ridiculed. Or as in the case of Lazarus, you'll find yourself surrounded by staff members, friends or co-workers in ministry who haven't got a clue as to what you're trying to convey to them.

Looking at the raising of Lazarus again, it was painfully obvious that when Jesus was speaking Faith to describe the situation, and His assignment from God, His own men didn't understand what He was talking about. They thought Jesus was talking about Lazarus taking a nap, while He was speaking about his death. Finally, after realizing that His staff just wasn't "getting it," He plainly came out and said, "Lazarus is dead." He didn't want to declare that, or even mention death in His conversations with His disciples, but in a moment of total exasperation He finally just came out and told them their friend was already dead.

Is it wrong to admit the truth like that? No, of course not! Jesus did it, so we know it's all right to admit the obvious. It's okay to admit there's a lower level of truth, but when talking the language of Faith, you understand the importance of expressing yourself with words that give God something to work with! By speaking Faith, we give God the opportunity to create and protect His pipeline of provision, power, and protection on our behalf, as we work to fulfill the Great Commission and "speak a word in season to him who is weary," as it says in Isaiah 50:4.

True, Lazarus was dead. True, the little 12-year-old girl was dead. But just admitting that doesn't elevate you to the level of communication that God can hook up with. Remember, God speaks Faith and no other language. He understands all the other spiritual languages we may speak, but He only responds to those who speak Faith. It's just that simple.

Jesus could've walked into the dead girl's house and begun weeping and wailing like all the rest of them. He could've sat down and cried over the death of His good friend, Lazarus. But He did something else. He met the bad news with words of Faith. He chose to speak and communicate at a higher level than what the circumstances indicated. He spoke Faith, even though He knew no one around Him understood the language being spoken. Even though He knew He'd be laughed at, ridiculed, maligned, misunderstood, and misinterpreted. So be it! If it happened to Jesus, you can be sure it will happen to you and me when we speak Faith. That's okay. Nothing wrong with that. It's wonderful when people hook up with you and join you in your declarations in Faith. But know this and remember it well—even if nobody understands where you're coming from, God does! And ultimately, He's the only one who needs to know!

PART TWO

Learning the Rules of the Language

ALL LANGUAGES HAVE RULES. WHETHER IT BE A
LANGUAGE OF THE HEAD OR A LANGUAGE OF THE HEART,
ALL LANGUAGES HAVE RULES THAT GOVERN THE
EXPRESSION OF THOUGHT. YOU DON'T JUST THROW
WORDS TOGETHER IN SOME HAPHAZARD WAY. NO, YOU
MUST LEARN THE RULES TO KNOW HOW TO ARRANGE
YOUR WORDS TO ACCURATELY EXPRESS YOUR THOUGHTS.
YOU MUST ALSO KNOW THE RULES WHICH SHOW YOU

HOW TO SPELL YOUR WORDS CORRECTLY, WHICH WORDS
TO USE TO EXPRESS YOUR THOUGHT, AND WHAT TENSE
YOU'RE SPEAKING IN. YOU MUST LEARN THE RULES AND
EVEN THE EXCEPTIONS TO THE RULES! IF YOU DON'T DO
THIS, YOU'LL NEVER BE ABLE TO MASTER ANY LANGUAGE,
WHETHER IT BE OF THE HEAD OR HEART.

THAT BEING THE CASE, LET'S BEGIN A LOOK AT SOME OF
THE BASIC RULES THAT GOVERN THE USAGE OF THE
LANGUAGE OF FAITH. I DON'T SUGGEST THE RULES WE
COVER IN THIS BOOK ARE THE ONLY ONES—THERE MAY
BE MORE. HOWEVER, IN THIS SECTION, WE WILL COVER
NINE RULES THAT ARE THE BASIC, FOUNDATIONAL,
FUNDAMENTAL RULES THAT ONE MUST LEARN AND
PRACTICE IN ORDER TO SPEAK FAITH FLUENTLY. LET'S
GET STARTED!

CHAPTER SEVEN

Rule 1:
Faith Says Only What
God Has Already Said

The first rule that governs the Faith language governs what we choose to say. First and foremost, we must learn that what God has said about our "problem" is all that needs to be said by us. Why? Because it's His Word that carries the power to change our situation and eliminate our problem. Our word apart from God's Word is basically powerless to change anything. It's what God has said that matters.

We say only what God has already said relative to the mountain, which represents the problem, situation, or circumstance that stands in our way. We find the promise or promises that cover our situation, and we speak it out of our mouths. Over and over, time and time again. For how long? Until the power released in God's spoken Word removes the obstacle, hurdle, mountain, problem, situation—whatever!

We want to be as smart as Balaam—before he later fell away and lost God's anointing.

> *Then Balaam answered and said to the servants of Balak, "Though Balak were to give me his house full of silver and gold, I could not go beyond the word of the LORD my God, to do less or more."*
>
> —NUMBERS 22:18

What a piece of great advice he gives us here! Don't go beyond the Word of the Lord, to do less or more. The principle remains as powerful now as it was the day Balaam declared it. Our first responsibility relative to using God's language of Faith? Say what He has already said. Take the pressure off of yourself. You don't have to be creative with what you're saying about the "situation" you're facing. You don't need to be!

God has already foreseen the problem you're facing, and He's already provided the promise that has the power to bring deliverance and victory. All you, or anyone, has to do is find the promise, believe it in your heart and speak it out your mouth. That's how it works!

> *If you confess with your mouth the Lord Jesus and believe in your heart that God has raised Him from the dead, you will be saved. For with the heart one believes unto righteousness, and with the mouth confession is made unto salvation.*
>
> —ROMANS 10:9-10

With the heart we believe, and with the mouth we confess unto—unto what? Unto whatever it is we need from God. Look at what Romans 1:17 says. For the gospel of Christ is the power of God unto salvation to all who believe. Notice that statement carefully. *The Gospel of Christ is the power of God unto salvation.* In the Greek, the word "salvation" is "*sozo.*" It means salvation from Hell, as well as deliverance from sickness, poverty, and mental oppression—basically, from all the works of the devil and works of the flesh that came upon us as a result of the fall of Adam.

The Gospel is God's power. It's not a portion of His power, it is His power. I heard a great evangelist, T.L. Osborn, once say that the secret to the power manifested in his crusades was simply announcing the promises to the people! He said something I've never forgotten. He said, *The Power is in the announcement!* What a great truth! A great truth that most of us know very little about. If we did have more understanding of this truth, we'd be far more careful with the words coming out of our mouths!

That's why, from Genesis to Revelation, the Bible is a book about words. More specifically, spoken words! How do we receive salvation? Believing with our hearts and saying something with our mouths! The principle applies to everything God has created and put into motion in this world. Spoken words release power. And as we've already discovered, language is all about verbal communication. Whether we're speaking a head language or a heart language, we're speaking! Remember that and never forget it! Knowing this, and walking in the light of it, makes all the difference in this world. We can walk in the fullness God intended for us if we learn to speak correctly, according to the promises and truths found in the Bible.

God's Word is creative in nature. His Word contains His power, but that power lies dormant until spoken in faith. When spoken in faith, it becomes the Faith language! Whether He's the one speaking it, or someone like you or me, when God's Word is spoken in faith, the power within it is released on behalf of the one doing the speaking. That's why you don't have to come up with some "original" declaration of freedom from your problems. Just say what God has already said, and His power will be put to work on your behalf for His glory. It's so simple we stumble over the simplicity of it!

Just find what God has said over your situation and start saying it. Granted, you might not be convinced of its power at first, but keep saying it anyway. That's the difference between the confession unto faith and the confession of faith. The confession unto faith is the process of declaring God's Word until it settles deep down in your heart and you're fully persuaded of its life-changing power. The confession of faith is when you speak that promise out of your heart, knowing that what you say will come to pass!

It's the mother of 2 Kings chapter 4 speaking about her dead son. It's Jesus at the funeral in Mark chapter 5 telling the family and friends the little girl was only sleeping. It's Jesus telling His staff that Lazarus was taking a nap in John chapter 11. It's you speaking God's Word over your situation, firmly convinced that what you say will come to pass.

> *"For assuredly, I say to you, whoever says to this mountain, 'Be removed and be cast into the sea,' and does not doubt in his heart, but believes that those things he says will be done, he will have whatever he says."*
>
> —MARK 11:23

Jesus didn't say you shall have what you think. He said you'll have what you say. He also didn't say you shall have what you really meant! How many times do you hear people say, "Well, I really didn't mean what I just said!" Well, that may salve your conscience and make you feel like you've just let yourself off the hook, but understand the rules of Faith don't operate by what you meant or by what you thought. The language of Faith has rules—and the first rule is that if you want God at work with you in your life, say what He says! Don't just think it. Say it! Don't just imply it. Say exactly what He's already said or, at the very least, say only what agrees with what He's already said. It's not what you thought or what you meant to say. It's what you said that works rule number one!

Listen to Jesus, and you'll hear Him expound upon this rule in His own sermons, messages, parables and conversations.

> *"For I have not spoken on My own authority; but the Father who sent Me gave Me a command, what I should say and what I should speak."*
>
> —JOHN 12:49

What did Jesus say? Only what God told Him to say! Nothing more, nothing less. It sounds just like what Balaam declared back in the book of Numbers. If you really want to know the "secret" to Jesus' success in ministry, here it is. Actually, it's not a secret at all, but just seems so because we've never really understood the rule He's using relative to using the language of Faith. Jesus said what God told Him to say, and then had enough sense to close His mouth. He knew there was a time to speak and a time to be silent. He knew how to speak and how not to speak. He knew where to speak and where not to speak. God told Him what, where, how, and to whom! After that, He was disciplined enough to keep His mouth shut. We should learn to do the same! Remember when Pilate was interrogating Him?

> *The Jews answered him, "We have a law, and according to our law He ought to die, because He made Himself the Son of God." Therefore, when Pilate heard that saying, he was the more afraid, and went again into the Praetorium, and said to Jesus, "Where are You from?" But Jesus gave him no answer. Then Pilate said to Him, "Are You not speaking to me? Do You not know that I have*

power to crucify You, and power to release You?" Jesus answered, "You could have no power at all against Me unless it had been given you from above. Therefore the one who delivered Me to you has the greater sin.'

—JOHN 19:7-11

Notice how Jesus exercised verbal discipline in this conversation with Pilate. At one point He knew it was best to keep quiet. At another point He knew it was best to answer. How did He know when to speak and when not to? God was telling Him! He was listening and saying only what God told Him to say, when God told Him to say it.

No, that doesn't make us robots! What it makes us is wise! God's not out to control us like some divine puppeteer pulling our strings down here on earth. No! We have been given the greatest gift of all—free will! But God sees our lives from His perspective and knows what is best for us at every turn. If He's telling us what to say, when to say it, how to say it, and who to say it to, He's got our best interest at heart—always! If God be for us, who can be against us (Romans 8:31)?

Do not answer a fool according to his folly, lest you also be like him. Answer a fool according to his folly, lest he be wise in his own eyes.

—PROVERBS 26:4-5

You see from this passage in Proverbs that there's a time to communicate and a time not to. Sometimes you engage the fool in conversation, sometimes you don't. God knows when it's best to do which, and we need to develop the inner sensitivity and discipline to hear His Spirit and then obey His Spirit. Nothing more, nothing less, just like Balaam said! This is the first rule governing the Faith language. *Say what God has already said!*

This is why it says in Romans 10:17 that "faith comes by hearing, and hearing by the Word of God." If faith comes by hearing, that means someone has to be speaking it. Either you're speaking it to yourself, or you're listening to someone else speak it. Not just thinking it, but speaking it. Thinking about the Word of God is great, and there's nothing wrong with that. It's good to always occupy our minds with God's Word. But if it's the language of Faith we're talking about, and working the rules that govern the language, understand that in order for the language to work, the Word of God must be spoken.

It's the spoken Word of God that carries the power to change your situation, break those sinful habits, overcome the lusts of the flesh and all the other junk we've got to contend with while living in these dead-to-sin bodies, in this sin-tainted world, which is run and controlled by the devil. To overcome it takes an inner realization that just loving God isn't enough for victory in our lives day in and day out. If you expect to be "more than a conqueror" (Romans 8:37) every day of your life, you must take the promises of God, put them in your heart, and speak them out of your mouth, believing that when spoken, the power within that Word is being released and put to work to change your situation.

> *Then Jesus said to them, "When you lift up the Son of Man, then you will know that I am He, and that I do nothing of Myself; but as My Father taught Me, I speak these things."*
>
> —JOHN 8:28

Who was our Lord's teacher? God. What did Jesus speak? What God taught Him to say. Can it be any more clear than that? That's why He was so successful and triumphant in His earthly ministry, and that's why we'll be as well in our earthly ministries. The good news is that Jesus didn't utilize any laws, rules, or principles we can't tap into right now, wherever we are. If He had done that, Satan could stand before God and declare the entire exercise a fraud! No, my friend. Everything Jesus did on earth He did as a man, anointed by God, instructed by God, empowered by God, and directed by God. That's why He's called the last Adam (1 Corinthians 15:45). He had to pass the test the first Adam failed, and if He got to use special powers, have access to special favor from God, enjoy some measure of privilege reserved only for Him, then once again the devil could cry foul, and legitimately so!

> *"I speak what I have seen with My Father, and you do what you have seen with your father."*
>
> —JOHN 8:38

> *Then Jesus answered and said to them, "Most assuredly, I say to you, the Son can do nothing of Himself, but what He sees the Father do; for whatever He does, the Son also does in like manner."*
>
> —JOHN 5:19

If you want to discipline yourself to speak and do only what God has already said and done, discipline yourself to spend time with God. There's no substitute for this. How could Jesus say that He speaks and does only what He has "seen" with His Father? Because the Lord spent hours in prayer communing with God, getting the instructions and directions for whatever the next step was in His ministry's assignment. How many times do we read in the Gospels about Jesus going off somewhere to pray—while His staff caught some zzz's under a tree somewhere? They'd wake up and look around for Jesus—unaware that He had been off behind some rock since 3 a.m., talking and fellowshipping with God.

Someone might say, "Well, that was just Jesus!" As if that lame, worn-out excuse is going to wash with God! No, Jesus said the works He did were to be the works we do (John 14:12), and therefore, we must learn the language of Faith like He learned it. How? By prioritizing our day and putting our time with God first—not last! Time with God is not supposed to be an afterthought, an asterisk at the end of our busy day. Rather, it's supposed to be the highlight of the day—every day! If Christians spent the kind of time with God that Jesus did, we'd see the results of that quickly enough! We'd be people walking, talking, and breathing Faith just like Jesus did! You can't spend quality time with God and not come away stronger, more dedicated, more focused—and more instructed on the language of Faith. It just comes with being in His presence.

> *"I can of myself do nothing. As I hear, I judge; and My judgment is righteous, because I do not seek My own will but the will of the Father who sent Me."*
>
> —JOHN 5:30

As Jesus listened to God, He received the counsel and guidance to know what to say, what to do and how to judge righteously. No matter how sticky the situation was that the devil tried to ensnare Him with, He always had the brilliant answer to confound His enemies and deliver the innocent. Nothing ever caught Him off guard. The woman caught in the act of adultery, as described in John 8:3-11, would certainly agree! Unexpectedly, He found Himself holding her life in His hands. Depending upon His answer, she would either be stoned to death or released. His answer to her accusers literally saved her life.

Then, in Luke 20:22-26, there was the question about whether to pay taxes to Caesar or not. Again, His answer absolutely dumbfounded His enemies and left them speechless! Also, remember John 7:32-46, where the Pharisees had sent officers to arrest Jesus, and after listening to Him teach, came back to their employers empty-handed. When asked why they hadn't arrested Him, they replied, "No man ever spoke like this Man." Imagine that! They go out to arrest Him and end up on His mailing list! Sent to apprehend Him, but end up buying all His books and CDs, becoming monthly partners with His ministry! Why? Because of what they heard! He spoke only what God had already said! Time and again, He just knew what to say, how to say it, when to say it and who to say it to. He was operating the first rule that the Faith language is built upon.

When are we going to learn this? It is the Word of God, spoken and declared in simple faith, that has the power to move any mountain we face. In that sense, Jesus was no different than you and I. The difference was found in how much time He spent in His Father's presence—listening, asking questions, receiving input and direction. He was sanctified through time spent with God, and therefore, His words and actions were always guided by the Holy Spirit. He was the perfect example of what the Word tells us in 1 Peter.

> *But sanctify the Lord God in your hearts, and always be ready to give a defense to everyone who asks you a reason for the hope that is in you, with meekness and fear.*
>
> —1 PETER 3:15

If we sanctify ourselves unto God the way Jesus did, we'll also be able to be "instant" in season as well as out of season (2 Timothy 4:2)! Through our time spent with God, we'll be well able to utilize rule number one—day in and day out, no matter where we are, who we're with, or what kind of "impossible" situation we find ourselves facing.

What Is the Devil Really Afraid Of?

This is what the devil is really afraid of. Not you, not me, and not any other Christian living on planet earth. He hates us, but really, he's not afraid of us per se. What he's really afraid of is the Word of God in us! He knows that the more time we spend with God in prayer and study of His Word, the more of His Word will be coming out our mouths. And as we speak God's Word, the power released is a power he has no answer for and is no match for. Therefore, when he attacks us, understand why he's attacking. It's to prevent us from using the language of Faith— which displays a faith based upon the exceedingly great and precious promises of God.

The devil isn't afraid of the Christian, but he's deathly afraid of the Word of God within us! Knowing that out of the abundance of the heart the mouth will speak, his prime objective is to prevent us from speaking the living Word of God that will ultimately "cook his goose," while at the same time giving God another avenue of expression through us here in the earth.

That's why when learning the rules that govern the Faith language, rule number one is rule number one! It starts here. Failure to understand this rule will basically negate the usage of the rest of the rules. We must all understand that.

Just say what God has said. Find it, repeat it, and keep on repeating it. How long? For as long as it takes. Ephesians 6:13 says that having done all to do to stand— stand! Stand, and keep on standing! Say God's Word and keep on saying it. It might take one year, saying God's Word hundreds or even thousands of times, before victory is achieved. But if that's the case, so be it. I always tell people who seem so concerned about how long this process will take, what's the rush!? Where are we going that we should be so concerned about "how long" this will take? If we're in God's perfect will, we can just relax knowing that His will is going to be done in our lives, and the timing of every manifestation is better left in His hands and not ours. Well, what about bills that are due on certain dates? Or sicknesses that seek to take our lives? What? God doesn't know these things? God needs to be informed about when our rent is due—as if He doesn't know? God needs to be informed about the seriousness of the illness we're having to deal with—as if He doesn't know?

Of course He's aware of everything going on in our lives. Jesus addressed this so well when, in Matthew 6:27, He asked which of you by taking thought can add one cubit to his stature? In other words, quit worrying about "how long" the process will take. God knows you and loves you more than you could ever know. In Matthew 10:30, Jesus also said the very hairs on our head are numbered! That ought to tell us to slow down and cast all our cares over to Him, knowing He cares for us (1 Peter 5:7)! You see, this is not just a flash-in-the-pan procedure that we utilize for a quick fix, and then it's back to a carnal, undisciplined, unsanctified life as usual, a life of verbal abuse and conversational laziness. No!

I remember a pastor in the Philippines once told me that as far as he was concerned, the message of faith was nothing more than a spiritual "parachute," something to use when we've tried everything else, nothing has worked, and we've basically fallen out of the plane, heading towards the fatal crash! Nothing could be farther from the truth! This is not some kind of "parachute." It's a way of life—in the same way that using the English language for an American is a way of life. It's something he or she will be using every day for the rest of their lives. So it is with Faith. God wants all of us to come to the place where, spiritually, we're speaking Faith as unconsciously as we do English! We're not even thinking about it—we're just doing it! When we get to that point, we've become fluent in Faith, and that's the goal all of us should have if we have the desire to be pleasing to God.

CHAPTER EIGHT

Rule 2:
Faith Works Best on the Principles of Synergy

But the LORD came down to see the city and the tower which the sons of men had built. And the LORD said, "Indeed the people are one and they all have one language, and this is what they begin to do; now nothing that they propose to do will be withheld from them. Come, let us go down and there confuse their language, that they may not understand one another's speech." So the LORD scattered them abroad from there over the face of all the earth, and they ceased building the city.

—GENESIS 11:5-8

This story from the book of Genesis reveals some powerful truths which we must understand if we're to master the language of Faith. When people get together and unify their speech and declare the same thing, a measure of spiritual force is created that can do much more than any one individual's effort could accomplish. This is amply illustrated in the incident that took place here at the Tower of Babel.

Notice that God is concerned with what is going on at the tower because, according to Him, they are all with one language, and because of that, whatever they set out to accomplish will be accomplished, whether it be the will of God or not! The point is that when men get together and begin saying the same thing, their ability to achieve desired results becomes much more attainable, reasonable, and possible.

So to speak Faith fluently, we must understand rule number two. Faith works best in an atmosphere of synergy, which is what we see taking place at the Tower of Babel. Now in case you don't know what synergy is, let me give you a dictionary definition. According to *The American Heritage Dictionary*, synergy is defined as:

> syn•er•gy \'sin-er-je\ n., pl. syn•er•gies. 1. The inter-action of two or more agents or forces so that their combined effect is greater than the sum of their individual effects. 2. Cooperative interaction among groups, especially among the acquired subsidiaries or merged parts of a corporation, that creates an enhanced combined effect. [From Greek *sunergia*, cooperation, from *sunergos*, working together. See SYNERGISM.]

Notice the first definition especially. Synergy is the interaction of two or more agents or forces so that their combined effect is greater than the sum of their individual effects. Here are some words pulled from the dictionary's thesaurus to give you an idea of what synergy is all about:

Joint work toward a common end

Collaboration

Cooperation

Joint effort

Teamwork

Joint action.

Pulling together

Participation

That's a powerful principle! If you want a scriptural example of synergy, look at Deuteronomy chapter 32.

> *How could one chase a thousand, and two put ten thousand to flight, unless their Rock had sold them, and the LORD had surrendered them?*
>
> —DEUTERONOMY 32:30

I've heard people and preachers quote that verse ever since I first was born again back in September of 1978. One can put a thousand to flight, and two can put ten thousand to flight. What is that? It's synergy! If we were talking about energy, we'd say that one can put a thousand to flight, and two can put two thousand to flight. One thousand plus one thousand equals two thousand. But that's not synergy. Synergy is when two or more "agents or forces" get together to produce far more strength, potential, and results than whatever they could do individually.

Have you ever been to a horse-drawn wagon pull? I have, and it's amazing to watch synergy at work when a team of horses starts pulling a weighted wagon down a set course against the clock. I used to live in Bowling Green, located in western Ohio, where every summer our town would host the county fair. And every year, one of the main events was the horse-drawn wagon pull. They would weigh down the wagon with as much as they could, then hitch up a team of horses and see which team could pull the weighted wagon farther and faster than the other competing teams. I can distinctly remember the announcer giving the spectators the weight of the wagon and what each horse had been able to pull individually. Then they'd hitch them together, and suddenly, they were able to pull much more than what each horse had pulled separately. That's synergy. Two agents or forces which, when working together, can generate much more strength together than they could alone.

In our case, the "agents or forces" would be people, not horses. And when learning the rules of Faith, remember that there is power in unified speaking. In case you didn't know it, that's why the prayer of agreement is such a powerful prayer!

> *"Again I say to you that if two of you agree on earth concerning anything that they ask, it will be done for them by My Father in heaven."*
>
> —MATTHEW 18:19

Many of us have read right over that tremendous promise and not given it a second thought. But we need to appreciate the power that can be produced when we pray the prayer of agreement. Why? Because the agreement in prayer produces an atmosphere of spiritual synergy, enabling those that pray it to do more and accomplish more than anything they achieve or receive on their own.

Now don't misunderstand me here. Your faith will work if you're the last person on the planet. It will work for anybody who dares to take God at His Word and act on it in simple faith. No matter who you are or where you are or what kind of impossible situation you may face in life, your faith will produce for you if you choose to stand. All of Hell may be against you. All your family may be against you. All your friends may be against you. But if you're bound and determined to see it through to victory through faith in God and His Word, you'll see the manifestation in your life. No doubt about it.

But as much as our faith can accomplish when we stand alone, it's much more powerful if it gets coupled with others who share the same faith and have the same passion and conviction as we do. Remember, Paul said we're debtors to the world (Romans 1:14), and as such, we must never forget that our lives are not about how much we can acquire or accumulate. Instead, our lives are to be living channels of His power, anointing, provision, and protection to others all around us. When it comes to using our faith, it's not about us. It's about us partnering with God to go out and turn this world upside down in the Name of Jesus. It's not about us, and it's not about God. It's about me *and* God—working together to fulfill the Great Commission. My part is to do what I can and use my faith to believe that God will do what I can't do. God will do what I can't do if I do what I can do; and what I can do is believe!

It's not that God can't respond to our faith when we're standing all alone—it's just that the way He's set things up gives those who can work together the advantage. The way of the spirit world is the way of unity. That's the way God set it up because that's the way He wants it. The body of Christ is one body with many parts. Romans says it this way:

> *For as we have many members in one body, but all the members do not have the same function, so we, being many, are one body in Christ, and individually members of one another. Having then gifts differing according to the grace that is given to us, let us use them.*

> —ROMANS 12:4-6

You can study 1 Corinthians 12:12-27 as well, which develops the same thoughts as what we find here in Romans chapter 12. In order to use the gifts we've been given responsibly and effectively, we must understand the importance of faith functioning best on the principles of synergy. One body, but many parts, doing different things in different parts of the world, but—and it's a big "but"—we must never forget that we're all supposed to be working together. Why? To create the synergy needed to fulfill the Great Commission with greater speed, power and anointing. Time is short, and if ever this principle was needed to help us, it's now! This is what Paul was talking about in his letter to the Ephesians.

> *And He Himself gave some to be apostles, some prophets, some evangelists, and some pastors and teachers, for the equipping of the saints for the work of ministry, for the edifying of the body of Christ, till we all come to the unity of the faith and of the knowledge of the Son of God, to a perfect man, to the measure of the stature of the fullness of Christ; that we should no longer be children, tossed to and fro and carried about with every wind of doctrine, by the trickery of men, in the cunning craftiness of deceitful plotting, but, speaking the truth in love, may grow up in all things into Him who is the head -Christ -from whom the whole body, joined and knit together by what every joint supplies, according to the effective working by which every part does its share, causes growth of the body for the edifying of itself in love.*
>
> —EPHESIANS 4:11-16

It's tragic that the body of Christ has spent centuries in abject failure when it comes to the daily application of the truths found in the passage we've just read. Notice we're talking in this passage about the unity of the faith, the importance of speaking the truth in love, with every part of the body doing its part. Why? So that the body may grow, mature, and continually reenergize itself for the glory of God and for the effective furtherance of the Gospel world-wide. This is the power of spiritual synergy, and it's one of the basic rules governing the language of Faith,

Now you can see why the devil works so hard to disrupt and destroy marriages. And if he tries so hard to destroy any marriage, imagine how hard he tries to destroy the Christian marriage! The devil knows that the believing husband and wife make two, and if they can ever get together on the same page about what they're speaking over and speaking about, no demon in Hell would be able to stop them from maximizing and realizing their fullest potential in Christ. Add to that sons and daughters who join up with their parents to speak the Word of God in unity of the faith, and all the more synergy is produced. The family unit was, and is, designed by God to be the source of synergy needed to take this world by storm! In reading Paul's writings, you can easily see how important he thought synergy was.

> *Now I plead with you, brethren, by the name of our Lord Jesus Christ, that you all speak the same thing, and that there be no divisions among you, but that you be perfectly joined together in the same mind and in the same judgment.*
>
> —1 CORINTHIANS 1:10

We see Paul admonishing the Romans to say the same thing among themselves. We see him doing the same with the Corinthians, and here's how he presented it to the Philippians:

Fulfill my joy by being likeminded, having the same love, being of one accord, of one mind. Let nothing be done through selfish ambition or conceit.

—PHILIPPIANS 2:2-3

You can't be of "one mind" and be in "one accord" if you're not all speaking the same thing! So if you intend to develop proficiency in Faith, get busy hooking up with those of like precious faith (2 Peter 1:1). Tap into the power of synergy and watch faith produce far more than what it could if you were standing on your own.

This is, as I've said, especially important for husbands and wives. Husbands, get with your wives and make sure you're both saying the same things about your marriage, your spiritual walk with God, your children, your finances, your employment, your careers, your health, your retirement—everything! Wives, do the same with your husbands. Parents, do your best to train your kids to join in and add their faith to yours, and thus create all the more synergy which God can utilize for you and through you to others.

CHAPTER NINE

Rule 3: Faith Is Spoken in the Present Tense

Blessed be the God and Father of our Lord Jesus Christ, who has blessed us with every spiritual blessing in the heavenly places in Christ.

—EPHESIANS 1:3

The third rule that governs the language of Faith deals with the tense of our declarations. The three main tenses we'll look at here are past, present, and future. You understand, of course, that if you get into a deeper study of language expression, you'll find there are many additional tenses besides past, present, and future. But for our discussion here, relative to our study of the language of Faith, we'll just look at the three main tenses most people are familiar with.

When we talk Faith, we always make our declarations in the present tense. Not past tense and not future tense. Always present tense. Why? Because, as we see from verses like Ephesians 1:3, our faith is always based upon something

God has already done! Not going to do, but already done. You see, when Jesus rose from the dead, He completely and totally defeated Satan. Through Jesus, God has already done everything He's ever going to do as far as our well-being is concerned. No stone was left unturned. Jesus did it all. He defeated Satan lock, stock, and barrel, and then made the spoils of that victory available to anyone who chooses to embrace it by faith.

That's what the word "salvation" really means in the Greek language. The Greek word for salvation is *sozo*, and according to *Vine's Expository Dictionary of New Testament Words*, as well as *Strong's Exhaustive Concordance*, it means healing, restoration to health, deliverance from demonic oppression, and victory over anything that would seek to prevent the recipient from walking in the fullness of what Jesus died to provide. So our salvation includes many things besides just being saved from Hell. It includes health and healing. It includes financial prosperity. It includes freedom from mental illness and demonic torment. It includes victory over fear. That's what all those "exceedingly great and precious promises" are all about—walking in the fullness of the blessings of God in Christ (2 Peter 1:1).

When we read those promises and choose to embrace them, our Faith declarations are delivered and spoken in the present tense. The reason for this is simple. Take healing as an example. First Peter 2:24 says that by the stripes of Jesus we were healed. That's past tense. Something that God has already done in Christ. So if I was healed by the stripes of Jesus, I am healed by the stripes of Jesus now! Present tense.

Getting back to Ephesians 1:3, it says that we're to bless God because He has blessed us with every spiritual blessing in Christ. If He has blessed us, that's past tense. So if He already has done it, then we've got those blessings now!

Present tense. How many spiritual blessings has God given us in Christ? It says "every" spiritual blessing has been made available to those who are in Christ. Every means all! Not some of them, but all of them. Every good and perfect gift has come down to us from God through Jesus (James 1:17). Not most of them, or a few of them, but all of them. And it's already done! Many Christians talk about God's blessings in a way that indicates their lack of understanding in this area. They talk about what God is going to do, as if it's something He's not done yet. That's not how you use the language of Faith!

God's not going to do one more thing for you or me or anybody. The work was done in Christ and is now available to anyone who chooses to enter into those blessings by faith. How do we enter in? By believing with our hearts and confessing with our mouths.

> But what does it say? "The word is near you, in your mouth and in your heart" (that is, the word of faith which we preach): that if you confess with your mouth the Lord Jesus and believe in your heart that God has raised Him from the dead, you will be saved. For with the heart one believes unto righteousness, and with the mouth confession is made unto salvation.
>
> —ROMANS 10:8-10

Notice how we enter in and enjoy the work of salvation. We believe with our hearts, and we say something with our mouths. Believe with the heart, speak with the mouth. This is how we receive our salvation and become born-again children of God. This is also how we receive every spiritual blessing that God has provided for us in Christ. We believe with our hearts, and we declare it with our mouths. Believing with the heart and speaking with the mouth is how the language of Faith is expressed.

What tense do we use when we speak? Present tense. In our hearts, we believe that God has already secured our victory and met our need, whatever that need may be. No matter what obstacle, hurdle, roadblock, mountain, problem, or situation you're facing in life, or will ever face, there is a promise or promises from God's Word that covers your situation. Meaning to say, you believe that God has already done something about the problem you're facing, and because of that, you declare with your mouth that you have the victory now! Philemon calls that the "effective sharing of your faith."

> *I thank my God, making mention of you always in my prayers, hearing of your love and faith which you have toward the Lord Jesus and toward all the saints, that the sharing of your faith may become effective by the acknowledgment of every good thing which is in you in Christ Jesus.*
>
> —PHILEMON 1:4-6

Notice here that if we're to share our faith effectively, we recognize and acknowledge every good thing which is already in us by way of the New Birth. We're not acknowledging things that aren't yet ours, but rather, acknowledging things that we've already got in Jesus. Therefore, our Faith declarations must be in the present tense. Not the past and not the future. The language of Faith is always based on what God has already done—not on what He's going to do. Therefore, it's always communicated in the present tense.

What about hope? If you want to talk future tense, that's hope! And there's nothing wrong with doing that. In fact, the Bible encourages us to express our hope whenever possible.

> *Let us hold fast the confession of our hope without wavering, for He who promised is faithful.*
>
> —HEBREWS 10:23

The Word of God exhorts us to hold fast the declaration of our hope without wavering. To do that we must speak in the future tense because that's what hope is. It's the mental image of victory. The mental image of answered prayer. It's using our imagination to create mental images that compliment our present tense declarations of faith. Faith and hope must work together, because Hebrews 11:1-3 tells us that faith is the substance of what we hope for. If there's no hope, there's nothing for our faith to give substance to. However, to use the language of Faith properly, you must understand the difference between faith and hope and the different tenses that are used to express them both.

Hope always deals with the future. Faith always deals with the present. Paul addressed this when he wrote to the Roman church.

> *Not only that, but we also who have the firstfruits of the Spirit, even we ourselves groan within ourselves, eagerly waiting for the adoption, the redemption of our body. For we were saved in this hope, but hope that is seen is not hope; for why does one still hope for what he sees? But if we hope for what we do not see, we eagerly wait for it with perseverance.*
>
> —ROMANS 8:23-25

When Paul talks about what we "see" and what we don't "see," he's talking about the difference between faith and hope. What does it mean when he says "hope that is seen is not hope"? It means that when the answer comes, or what we commonly call our "manifestation," there is no need for hope anymore. In Hebrews 6:19, hope is referred to as an anchor of the soul. In 1 Thessalonians 5:18, it's called a helmet. Why an anchor, and why a helmet? Because hope always deals with the future—talking about things that haven't yet happened or come to pass in this world of ours.

That's why the return of Jesus is called the "blessed hope" (Titus 2:13). Why is it a blessed hope? Because it's a promise from God that hasn't happened yet. It will happen, but not yet. To think and talk about how wonderful it will be when our Lord returns—that's a profession of our hope. That's what it's talking about in 1 Peter 1:3 when the Bible tells us that we've been born again to a living hope through the resurrection of Jesus.

We do the same thing when we declare our faith in the present tense. When we say that by the stripes of Jesus we are healed, hope fills our minds with the mental picture of us being well again. And when we talk, we can use both present tense declarations of Faith and future tense declarations of hope—the Bible tells us to do it. However, when it's Faith you're using to connect your situation with the power of God necessary to change your situation, it's always present tense declarations, please. Not past, and not future.

Do you have family members not yet serving God? Speak over them in the present tense. Say things like this: My husband loves the Lord with all his heart. He's filled with the Spirit and prays in tongues every day. My wife is on fire for the Lord. Our kids love going to church. They love reading their Bibles and spending time in prayer every day. Our kids love each other. They're kind, generous, thoughtful, and loving to each other. The peace of God rules and reigns in our home and in our family.

Got some problems with your kids in school with their grades? Use the language of Faith to change the situation. Remember, as long as they live under your roof, you've got parental authority over them, and God expects you to use it in the arena of Faith. Instead of always criticizing your kids for their poor grades or for having a bad learning attitude, use Faith to apply God's power and change the situation. But because it's Faith you're using, make sure the confessions are in the present tense. Say things like this: Our kids do well in school and get good grades consistently. The Holy Spirit gives them supernatural recall for tests, reports, assignments, homework, and whatever else they're responsible for. They set an example for Christian behavior which teachers and fellow students can see.

Use your present tense declarations of Faith over your job. If you don't like your job, start speaking in Faith to change the situation. If you think you're underpaid or under-appreciated, do something about it with your Faith! Instead of mumbling and complaining to fellow workers, family members, and even to your employer or supervisor, take the issue to God in prayer and begin declaring your present tense statements of Faith. Say something like this: I love my job. It's fulfilling and well-paying. My skills are utilized, and my supervisors appreciate and recognize the work I'm doing for the company.

What about your personal finances? Quit putting up with lack. Use the language of Faith to change what you see in the natural. I've always said that if you change what you say, what you say will change what you see. Tired of having more month than money at the end of the month? Look at your wallet and declare it is filled (present tense, please!) with all the money you need to pay your bills, save responsibly, and give abundantly towards the work of God.

Tired of all the chronic aches, pains, and sicknesses? Look at your body and declare it is not only healed from top to bottom, but healthy and whole too. If necessary, put your hands on areas of your body in need of healing. But always remember to say what you desire in the present tense.

Once again, it's perfectly all right to talk your hope by talking in the future tense about how wonderful it will be when the manifestation comes. But to use the Faith language to change or get rid of your "issue," "problem," "mountain," or whatever—always make your statements in the present tense.

Now that may seem hard at first, and it will certainly sound a bit awkward if you're not accustomed to doing it, but that's okay. The more you do it the more natural it will become to you, and in no time, you'll have developed the habit of working rule number three to your benefit time and time again.

CHAPTER TEN

Rule 4:
Faith Is a Language
of Joy

And being confident of this, I know that I shall remain and continue with you all for your progress and joy of faith.

—PHILIPPIANS 1:25

The joy of faith! If we're walking by faith and not by sight, as it tells us in 2 Corinthians 5:7, we should be joyful people. If the just are to live by faith, as it says in Romans 1:17, then we're supposed to be joyful people. Why? Because faith and joy go together and can't be separated. You can't be in faith and be joyless at the same time. It doesn't work that way.

If you want to know whether you're really in faith with God or not, check up on your joy! Throughout the New Testament, whenever you find faith under discussion, joy is close at hand. Why? Because joy is the natural result of your decision to walk by faith! And before I go any further with you, let me differentiate between joy and happiness. I'm not talking here about being happy. There's nothing wrong with being happy, as long as my happiness isn't connected to someone or something in violation of the Word of God. Sinners can be happy, but from a biblical perspective, only the Christian can be joyful. Why? Because joy is not a feeling. It's a fruit.

Galatians 5:22 mentions joy as one of the nine fruits listed. The fruit listed is not the fruit of the Holy Spirit. He doesn't need any fruit. It's the fruit of the born-again human spirit. Joy is one of nine fruits the human spirit is supposed to develop and cultivate after being born again. Of course, the Holy Spirit is within us to help us with this development, but it's not His fruit—it's our fruit.

In the Greek, the word for "spirit" isn't capitalized, the way it's translated into English by most modern English translations. It's just referred to as fruit of the spirit. But whose spirit? God's Holy Spirit or our human spirit? I believe it's the human spirit being discussed here, not God's Holy Spirit. Remember, Jesus referred to Himself as the vine and us as the branches. Fruit on a fruit tree doesn't grow on the trunk of the tree, does it? No, it grows on the end of the branch. We're the branches, not the Holy Spirit. The fruit growing in our lives is the fruit of our spirit, as it matures and becomes more sensitive to God and His Word.

Love, joy, peace, patience, kindness, goodness, faithfulness, gentleness, self-control. These are nine fruits of the recreated human spirit. Joy is called a fruit, not a feeling. Happiness is a feeling, a mood for the moment. It's something that changes all the time, depending upon the circumstances and situations of life. However, joy is unchanging. Joy isn't based upon external circumstances, but instead, is based upon the fact that we're in Christ and He's in us. *Joy is based on Jesus.* That's why we can have it when, in the natural, there's nothing to be joyful, or even happy, about. Jesus never changes, so our faith should never change, and because of that, our joy should be constant too.

So when we're talking about using the language of Faith, understand the importance of using it in the context of Christian joy! I mean after all, if we truly believe that God is in control of our lives, and if we truly believe that His Word is final authority in our lives, why wouldn't we be joyful all the time? Not just when we felt like it, but by faith, all the time! When things are going right, but also when things are going wrong! If you truly believe God's Word is the final word on the issue or challenge you're facing, and you know that He loves you and is for you and not against you (Romans 8:31), why wouldn't you be joyful all the time? Not just when the answers come, but before you see any visible indication that God is moving to respond to your faith in His Word. Why? Because like I said, our joy is not based on our feelings. It's based on Jesus, and He never changes, nor do His promises. That's why Paul makes this statement to the Philippians:

> *Rejoice in the Lord always. Again I will say, rejoice!*
> —PHILIPPIANS 4:4

The last time I checked, "always" means always! Always doesn't mean only when everything is going the way I want it to. Always means that no matter how things are going in my life, I'm to be walking by faith, not by sight, and that means that no matter how things are going—good or bad—I'm to be rejoicing! I just love these statements from God that leave no room for the flesh! Always means exactly what it says! Always! That's it. Beyond debate. Beyond discussion. Always! Are you a doer of this verse? Am I? Be truthful now—God knows!

If we're honest with ourselves, we'll all have to admit that there have been times when we haven't done what this verse tells us to do. But if we're ever to become fluent in Faith, we're going to have to start letting the power of joy hook up with the power of faith—the way God intended. Failure to do so will only hinder our efforts to speak the language of Faith.

Let's look at a few passages in the New Testament which illustrate the partnership between faith and joy.

> *Blessed be the God and Father of our Lord Jesus Christ, who according to His abundant mercy has begotten us again to a living hope through the resurrection of Jesus Christ from the dead, to an inheritance incorruptible and undefiled and that does not fade away, reserved in heaven for you, who are kept by the power of God through faith for salvation ready to be revealed in the last time. In this you greatly rejoice, though now for a little while, if need be, you have been grieved by various trials, that the genuineness of your faith, being much more precious than gold that perishes, though it is tested by fire, may be found to praise, honor, and glory at the revelation of Jesus Christ, whom having not seen you love. Though now you do not see Him, yet believing, you rejoice with joy inexpressible and full of glory, receiving the end of your faith—the salvation of your souls.*
>
> —1 PETER 1:3-9

In this great passage from 1 Peter, we see how faith and joy work together to produce the strength needed to face the testing, temptations, and trials of this life. If you read this passage in context, Peter is writing to encourage the believers to remain steadfast in faith to Christ, in spite of intense persecution that's coming against them. When Peter writes about their faith being "tested by fire," he's talking about the fires of persecution. These believers were being sorely tempted to renounce Christ and go back to the way they were before, because of the pressure of the persecution being applied against them.

But how does Peter encourage them to stay loyal to Jesus? By standing strong in faith through joy! Notice how the two are intertwined here. You can't be walking in one without walking in the other simultaneously. They go together. Read through and circle, highlight, or underline all the references to faith, and then do the same for all the references to joy. I'm especially fond of the phrase found in verse 8, which says: "yet believing, you rejoice with joy inexpressible." Look at that phrase carefully. Yet believing, you rejoice! Yet believing, you rejoice! Yet believing, you rejoice! Yet believing, you rejoice! Do you see it? If I'm truly "believing," I should be "rejoicing." If I'm not rejoicing, I'm not yet believing! I can't be believing if there is no rejoicing! Let that sink in for a minute!

Many of us have thought we were walking by faith and not by sight, when in fact we were nothing more than self-deceived, as it says in James 1:22. I myself, many times, have thought I was truly walking in faith, when in reality I was not at all—I just thought I was. Why? Because even though I was making all the right Faith statements, all the right Faith declarations, and all the right confessions, there was no joy! As I began to understand this particular rule that governs the Faith language, I began to see how self-deceived I had been. The same is true for so many believers out there who love the Lord, try to walk by faith, and become frustrated because the answers are not coming as they would like. In part, I believe it's because many of us are not tapping into the power of joy—not just as a fruit of our spirits, but as the one, true way to let the world know that we really and truly trust God and believe that His Word is final authority in our lives.

Let me say it to you this way. Joy is the external expression of our internal conviction. If I'm truly using my faith and believing God, how would anybody know that? Of course, God sees into my heart, but in terms of those around me, how would they know I'm walking by faith and using the language of Faith correctly? One of the best ways is with joy! That's what Peter was trying to get across to those he was writing to in the letter of 1 Peter. These people were being persecuted, and the pressure to renounce Jesus and go back to the old ways was great. To counter that attack, Peter implores them to stand strong in faith—by relying on the power of joy! Remember what he said: yet believing, you rejoice with joy inexpressible. He's telling them that if they want to hold fast their confession of faith, they're going to have to tap into the "inexpressible" force of joy!

James said the same things to those he wrote to. Let's see how he words it.

> *My brethren, count it all joy when you fall into various trials, knowing that the testing of your faith produces patience. But let patience have its perfect work, that you may be perfect and complete, lacking nothing. If any of you lacks wisdom, let him ask of God, who gives to all liberally and without reproach, and it will be given to him. But let him ask in faith, with no doubting, for he who doubts is like a wave of the sea driven and tossed by the wind. For let not that man suppose that he will receive anything from the Lord; he is a double-minded man, unstable in all his ways.*
>
> —JAMES 1:2-8

This passage in James is very similar to the passage from 1 Peter. In both cases, James and Peter write to encourage believers to "hang in there" and not fall away because of the intense persecution coming their way. James talks about "the testing of your faith." That's the same as Peter talking about their faith being tested "by fire." These brethren were under attack, and both apostles are writing to encourage them to stay strong, stay steadfast, and not fall away. How are they to do this? Through their faith—coupled with the power of joy!

Notice in both 1 Peter and James, the passages let us know that testing, trials, and temptation will come against us. Not maybe, but definitely! It's not a question of "if," but rather, a question of "when." Also, it's not just a question of "when," but "how severe"! That's why, when you look at faith verses in the Bible, you'll always find joy verses close by. The two will either be found in the same verse or in close proximity. They have to—they go together!

Remember that laughter, smiling, a certain "glow" about you—these are all signs that joy is at work down deep inside. It's true that if you're happy, you can be laughing and smiling too. But with joy, it's something from the inside, not something from the outside. When I'm speaking Faith, there should be a lot of smiling, laughing, running, jumping—you get the point! Not some superficial show of carnality, but a deep-seated conviction that God is in control. His Word works! If He is for me, nobody can be against me, and greater is He in me than the devil in the world. If God says that you can do all things through Christ who strengthens you (Philippians 4:13), and you believe it, then start letting God's joy be the outward expression of your inner conviction.

Rule 5:
Faith Is a Language of Peace

"Peace I leave with you, My peace I give to you; not as the world gives do I give to you. Let not your heart be troubled, neither let it be afraid."

—JOHN 14:27

If we're to learn the language of Faith, we must know it's a language that expresses itself in an environment of total peace and trust in Almighty God. No more stress. No more pressure. No more anxiety. No more enrollment in local "anger management" classes! No more impatience with God—or with men. Complete peace! Total peace! Wonderful peace! A peace that, as Jesus said, comes only from knowing God in Christ. There's no substitute and no alternative form of peace. The world doesn't have it, so they can't give it. It's found only in Jesus.

Notice in this passage, as Jesus was preparing His disciples for His passion and crucifixion, He told them not to let their hearts become troubled. If He told us not to let our hearts be troubled, then it's not up to God that we stay in peace, but up to us. And isn't that what faith is all about? Learning how to trust God, especially when things aren't going the way we want them to.

When we walk in faith, and speak the language of Heaven, we do so because we trust in God. We believe in Him. We have that confident assurance that if He be for us, who can be against us (Romans 8:31)? Therefore, the Faith language can't really be spoken in an atmosphere of fear, doubt, uncertainty, impatience, trepidation, or nervousness about the "outcome." When we speak Faith, we speak from a position of knowing. We don't just hope God comes through—we know He will. Of course, our minds will be a constant battlefield as we ward off the lies of the enemy. But deep down inside, down inside our hearts, we have that knowing. That intangible something—an awareness that God's Word will prevail in our lives.

If you read Hebrews chapters 3 and 4, you can clearly see the language of Faith under discussion. God is telling the readers that, back in the Old Testament, His people had the opportunity to embrace His promises, but chose instead to believe the majority report of doubt and unbelief. The result? God's angry and they're out in the wilderness wandering around, waiting for the unbelieving generation to pass away. Let's look at this passage and see what we can learn about how God's language of Faith is a language of peace.

> *Therefore, as the Holy Spirit says: "Today, if you will hear His voice, do not harden your hearts as in the rebellion, in the day of trial in the wilderness, where your fathers tested Me, tried Me, and saw My works forty years. Therefore I was angry with that generation, and said, 'They always go astray in their heart, and they have not known My ways,' so I swore in My wrath, 'They shall not enter My rest.'"*
>
> —HEBREWS 3:7-11

A couple of things to consider here before we read on. First, notice God was angry with His people. Why was He angry? Because they weren't walking in faith. They weren't talking Faith. They were walking and talking doubt and unbelief. Make a memo to yourself here: God gets angry when His people walk in doubt and unbelief. He always has, and He always will. This goes for you and me as much as for the Jews back then. God is a faith being, and He doesn't like it when we choose to lose our peace over situations or circumstances that He's well able to give us the victory over.

Secondly, notice God said they would not enter His rest! What is that? "His rest" is that special place where we live in the constant awareness of God's love, power, provision, protection, and promotion. We're at rest. We're not worried. We're not impatient. We're not "stressed out." We're at peace, restful, communing with the Lord our God. We have that confident, inner awareness that He's in control, and even more importantly than that, He loves us and wants to take good care of us. After all, doesn't 1 Peter 5:7 tell us to cast all our cares upon God, knowing He cares for us? Sure it does! Well, when speaking Faith, we're simply declaring our trust in God and announcing with our words that as far as we're concerned, all is well—no matter how bad things may look in the natural. Why? Because we've entered into "His rest." We're at peace. We're established in faith, and our language confirms it.

Let's keep reading. There's more!

> *Beware, brethren, lest there be in any of you an evil heart of unbelief in departing from the living God; but exhort one another daily, while it is called "Today," lest any of you be hardened through the deceitfulness of sin. . . . Now with whom was He angry forty years? Was it not with those who sinned, whose corpses fell in the wilderness? And to whom did He swear that they would not enter His*

rest, but to those who did not obey? So we see that they could not enter in because of unbelief.

—HEBREWS 3:12-13,17-19

Why were the Jews unable to enter into the rest of God? Because of their unbelief. It wasn't God that was stopping them, and it wasn't the devil either. It was their own doubt, unbelief, and fear. Remember what Jesus said. He said not to let our hearts be troubled. Obviously in this passage, we see that the Jews had definitely allowed their hearts to become troubled. Their wrong choice in this matter cost them 40 years of happiness, rest, joy, and blessings from God. Think about that!

You see, if I'm speaking Faith, I'm speaking it because I believe in something. I'm using Faith because I'm confident and convinced that God is my God, that He loves me, and that in Christ all things are possible to me if I choose to believe (Mark 9:23). I'm not wondering, hoping, wishing, or gambling that God will come through for me. I'm assured. I'm established. I'm at peace.

One of the best ways to check to see if you're really speaking Faith is to check your "peace barometer." The right words might be coming out of your mouth, but what's going on inside? Are you at peace? Are you established with God's Word in your heart? Oh, sure, the lies of the enemy will be persistent obstacles in your mind, and your body might jump in there, too, with symptoms that seem to mock your confession, but all that aside, are you firmly entrenched in your heart? Are God's promises the final authority as far as you're concerned? Not the word of the doctor or the word of the banker or the word of your employer or the word of some murdering terrorist somewhere. But God's Word—is it final authority for you? If it is, the language of Faith is the language you're speaking.

Therefore, since a promise remains of entering His rest, let us fear lest any of you seem to have come short of it. For indeed the gospel was preached to us as well as to them, but the word which they heard did not profit them; not being mixed with faith in those who heard it. For we who have believed do enter that rest.

—HEBREWS 4:1-3

We who speak Faith speak it because we have entered a place of rest that the world knows nothing about. It's a peace that Jesus said only He can give. If you've ever been there, you know how wonderful it is. I know in my own life, when I manage to get to a place of true faith, and I'm speaking it with firm conviction in my heart, it's an absolutely wonderful feeling! I feel so liberated. So peaceful! And that's what speaking Faith is all about. Peace! Spiritual tranquility! Spiritual rest!

Notice once again how God makes a point to let us know that the reason the Jews lost out was because they didn't mix faith with the promises He gave to them. They chose not to believe. Instead of speaking Faith, they chose to speak Fear, Doubt, and Unbelief. They mumbled and murmured and took themselves out of position to receive the blessings God had promised them. Too bad for them, and too bad for the multitude of Christians today who do the same thing! I hope you're not one of them!

With God's help, I pray I won't become one of them either! If there are promises out there that God wants me to enjoy, I want to enjoy them! How about you? I want His blessings, and I want to live in His rest. I want everything I say to be something that keeps Heaven's highway open on my behalf. I want to be fluent in Faith!

As we read on in Hebrews, it gets better!

There remains therefore a rest for the people of God. For he who has entered His rest has himself also ceased from his works as God did from His. Let us therefore be diligent to enter that rest, lest anyone fall according to the same example of disobedience.

—HEBREWS 4:9-11

Okay, let's see now. According to God, there is a rest promised to the people of God. Are you walking in that rest? Am I? Sad to say, many of us are not, and the language we speak gives us away. But if we're not, how do we get back in faith and enter into the rest promised by Almighty God? By doing what He says in these verses. We must cease from our own works! We must stop trying to solve our own problems and move to a place where we enter His rest and let God be God in our lives! It's like the difference between Martha and Mary in Luke's Gospel. Remember the difference between those two sisters?

Now it happened as they went that He entered a certain village; and a certain woman named Martha welcomed Him into her house. And she had a sister called Mary, who also sat at Jesus' feet and heard His word. But Martha was distracted with much serving, and she approached Him and said, "Lord, do You not care that my sister has left me to serve alone? Therefore tell her to help me." And Jesus answered and said to her, "Martha, Martha, you are worried and troubled about many things. But one thing is needed, and Mary has chosen that good part, which will not be taken away from her."

—LUKE 10:38-42

The difference between Martha and Mary is the difference between someone speaking Faith and someone speaking something else! You see, the more you spend time with Jesus, the more convinced you become that it's to your benefit to let Him run the show—not you! Most of us—myself included at times—are like Martha. We see the needs, the problems, the challenges, and off we go to solve them, with or without God's help. Most of the time without! And what happens? We end up like Martha. Upset. Worn out. Angry. Hurt. Offended. Sound familiar? It does to me! I've been there, too, many times.

But if I just step back and renew my mind to God's love and to His faithfulness in my life, if I just let my Faith do the talking and let God be God in my life, I become a Mary and no longer a Martha. I'm in faith, listening to the Master, speaking His language, believing His Word, expecting His promises to come to pass in my life. In peace. At rest. Praising God!

Note that Mary chose the good part. She chose to sit at Jesus' feet. She could've chosen to run back to the kitchen and help her sister, but that's not what she did. Instead, she saw the bigger picture and made the choice to receive the "good part." On the other hand, Martha chose to receive the "hard part"! Do you want the good part or the hard part? It's hard trying to serve God in the power of your own zealousness! Not only is it hard, it's really impossible. Why? Because we're facing an enemy who is very strong, organized, cunning, and patient against us. We have to learn that the weapons against him are not carnal, but spiritual (2 Corinthians 10:3-5). We have to learn to speak Faith from Mary's example of sitting at the Master's feet, instead of being like Martha, running all around, full of zeal without knowledge (Romans 10:2). That kind of zeal has no real power because it's based on the flesh, and the flesh is no match for the spiritual power the enemy is working with. We need God's faith, and we need His peace. Mary knew this. Martha didn't.

If you and I are to receive the "good part" in our lives today, we've got to enter into God's rest, enjoying the peace that only He can give. From there, our declarations of Faith will not just be some hollow attempt at convincing ourselves, but instead, our firm expression of what we truly believe.

Jesus Rose from the Dead to Provide Us with His Peace

I find it very interesting that after Jesus rose from the dead, each time He appeared to His disciples He gave them a salutation of peace. Go back and read it for yourself. Read John's Gospel, especially chapter 20. Three times in that chapter, in verses 19, 21, and 26, we see Jesus greeting His loved ones with a salutation of peace. Why? Of all the things He could've said, having just risen from the dead, isn't it interesting He chose to speak peace over His disciples?

I believe it's because that's what He died to provide us. God's peace. A legal peace first, and then a living peace after that. The legal peace came when He became our sin substitute, died in our place, and rose from the dead. Having put His precious blood on Heaven's mercy seat, a new covenant was ratified, and our redemption was complete. For you, for me, for all men for all time. That's our legal peace.

But then what? How do we walk that out daily? How do we live it each day? How do we let the world know we're one with Christ and complete in Him (Colossians 2:10)? By developing what I call a "living" peace. Taking my legal peace and turning it into a lifestyle that exudes the peace that only comes from a saving knowledge of our Lord Jesus Christ. To do that, I'm going to have to be speaking the language of Heaven, which is Faith. Every day, for the rest of my life. It's what Jesus did, and what you and I will have to do as well. It's not easy, but it's well worth the effort. It's what James was talking about when he talked about being single-minded on the Word of God.

> *But let him ask in faith, with no doubting, for he who doubts is like a wave of the sea driven and tossed by the wind. For let not that man suppose that he will receive anything from the Lord; he is a double-minded man, unstable in aft his ways.*
>
> —JAMES 1:6-8

The double-minded man is a man without peace in his life. He's upset, nervous, worried, and, as it says here, unstable in all his ways. Not just a few of his ways—but all of his ways! That means from morning until evening, from the time he wakes up until the time he goes to bed, he's basically a mental wreck. There's no peace. His language is that of Fear or Doubt or Unbelief or Uncertainty about the future. It's certainly not the language of Faith coming out of his mouth!

The single-minded man, however, is a man void of doubt about two things: God's ability, number one, and God's willingness, number two.

You see, plenty of people believe in God's abilities. "Oh, yes," they will say, "God can do anything." But ask these same people if they believe the God-who-can-do-anything is willing to use that ability to bring victory in their lives, and suddenly they're not so sure. It's called being double-minded. A man of two minds. A man who has a battle raging within and, at present, hasn't finally put God's Word where it should be in his mind—as final authority.

Yes, of course we know God is able to deliver us, help us, heal us, provide for us, anoint us, etc. But do you believe He's willing to use His powers on your behalf? That's what separates the single-minded man from the double-minded man. The single-minded man believes in both God's ability and His willingness. The double-minded man hasn't yet settled that issue in his head. And as a result, he's tossed to and fro (back and forth), like a wave of the sea! Instead of having a heart that is established in faith (see Psalm 112), he's got a heart that constantly vacillates between believing God's Word or believing the world's word.

But when I finally decide that God's Word is final authority, my language begins to reflect that. I speak words of Faith, no longer words of Fear. My communication becomes something God can work with, instead of something the devil can use against me. It's when I'm at peace with God's promises being for me, not just for humankind in general, that I can really begin speaking Faith with both conviction and authority.

So if you're speaking Faith, you're at peace! Peace with God and peace with your surroundings and circumstances. No more stress. No more worrying. No more emotional pressure. No more need for "anger management"! It's a wonderful place to be, and we can get there. It's not "Mission Impossible." Rather, it's "Mission Achievable!"

Bottom line is this: it takes no more effort to enter into God's rest and believe His Word than it does to stay worried and believe what everyone else says that contradicts God's promises in your life. The choice is up to you—not God. He already made His choice. Jesus was sent, then the Holy Spirit was sent, and now we're sent! Let's take God at His Word, enter into His rest, become single-minded on our Lord's promises, and speak the language of Faith. When we do that, we're in obedience to Hebrews 12:14, which says to "follow after peace." Let's follow after peace. Let's speak the language of Faith. (For a more in-depth study on this subject, refer to my book, *Divine Peace*.)

CHAPTER TWELVE

Rule 6:
Faith Is a Language
Which Speaks
the End Result

(As it is written, "I have made you a father of many nations") in the presence of Him whom he believed—God, who gives life to the dead and calls those things which do not exist as though they did.

—ROMANS 4:17

God calls things which do not exist as though they do exist. If He does it, it's okay for us to do the same. In fact, because we're made in His image and likeness, He expects us to do the same. Yet, if you attempt to do this around most people, you'll be branded as a liar. Or a nut case. Or whatever! But one thing is for sure—you certainly won't be applauded and congratulated for acting and speaking like God! Oh, no! To the contrary, you'll be laughed at. Ridiculed. Made fun of. Gossiped about behind your back. And these are church people I'm talking about—not the rank and file "sinners."

When you speak Faith, you're doing what God did with Abraham. Calling things that be not as though they were. In other words, you're speaking the "end result," not what contradicts the desired end result as you declare your Faith. Once again, if God does it, it's not lying! If it is, God's the biggest liar that ever came down the pike, and of course, we know that's not true!

Jesus spoke the end result when He said the little girl in Mark 5 was not dead, only sleeping. He did it again when He told His disciples that His good friend Lazarus was sleeping in John 11, when in fact he was really dead. The mother of the dead son in 2 Kings chapter 4 spoke the end result when she told the prophet all was well with her family as her son lay dead on the prophet's bed in her own house.

What are these examples of? Of people speaking the end result. Of people so filled with confidence and conviction in God, they speak not according to what they see at the moment, but what they expect to see when their victory will manifest—whatever that victory might mean.

To some, that means saying, "I'm healed," with symptoms and pain in a body that declares I'm sick and getting sicker. To others it means saying, "all my bills are paid, I've got money saved up for my children's education, I'm independent of the economy around me"—while staring at a wallet that has more family photos than money in it! Or while looking at a bank passbook that says "zero balance." To others, it means saying, "I have a great, well-paying career, a satisfying job"—while the economy is in the tank, there are no jobs in your area of interest or expertise, and you're driving a pizza delivery car!

Whatever it is to you, it means you call those things that be not as though they were—because that's what the language of Faith is all about. You see, from God's vantage point, everything we're using faith to obtain has already been made available in the spirit realm.

For we who have believed do enter that rest, as He has said: "So I swore in My wrath, 'They shall not enter My rest,'" although the works were finished from the foundation of the world.

—HEBREWS 4:3

When were the "works of God" finished? When someone handed you the money to pay the bills? When the healing manifested in your body? When you just got hired for that perfect position? No! From the foundation of the world! What does that mean? It means that as far as God is concerned, you were delivered, made complete, declared victorious, and anointed for success before the world was ever created! That's right! Before any of us were ever even born, God saw us and declared us triumphant in Christ!

Now, we may never achieve that if we choose to live below our rights and privileges in Christ, but if that's the case, it won't be God's fault! It will be ours! He's already declared the end result as far as He's concerned. And His declaration is one of victory, not one of defeat. You may see yourself as financially broke and down on your luck, but that is not how God sees you, and that's not how He's talking about you. He talks and thinks about you all the time, and has from before you were even born! Did you know that? That's what Psalms says.

Many, O Lord my God, are Your wonderful works which You have done; and Your thoughts toward us cannot be recounted to You in order; if I would declare and speak of them, they are more than can be numbered.

—PSALM 40:5

How precious also are Your thoughts to me, O God! How great is the sum of them! If I should count them, they would be more in number than the sand; when I awake, I am still with You.

—PSALM 139:17-18

God thinks of you more times than the number of grains of sand that cover all the beaches of the world! Whoa! That's a lot of thoughts! And what does He think about? Well, according to Jeremiah, His thoughts are good and pleasant.

For I know the thoughts that I think toward you, says the Lord, thoughts of peace and not of evil, to give you a future and a hope.

—JEREMIAH 29:11

What's He doing when He thinks of you so often? He's calling things that are not as though they are. Even if your life is not where it should be according to God's Word and His perfect will for your life, He is still going to be calling things that are not as though they were in your life. That's His way. God is always positive towards us, and as it says so well in Romans chapter 8, if God be for us, who can be against us? God is for us, not against us, so He's always going to be speaking something positive over our lives, no matter how things may appear in the natural at any given moment. Isn't that comforting? Thank God—I think it is! God knows my life is not always where it needs to be in terms of spiritual maturity and sanctification, but praise God, He sees me the way He's destined me to be, not the way I may be disappointing Him today.

He does the same with you and with all men. Thank God we serve a God like that!

Be Like Abraham: Fully Persuaded

We want to live like Abraham, who is called the father of our faith and a friend of God (see Romans 4:16 and James 2:23). What made him so pleasing to God was his faith— choosing to believe that what God had promised, He was able to perform.

> *And not being weak in faith, he did not consider his own body, already dead (since he was about a hundred years old), and the deadness of Sarah's womb. He did not waver at the promise of God through unbelief, but was strengthened in faith, giving glory to God, and being fully convinced that what He had promised, He was also able to perform.*
>
> —ROMANS 4:19-21

Okay. Abraham was fully convinced. The original *King James Version* says he was fully "persuaded." That means there was no doubt in his mind about whether God was going to be "good" for His Word or not. As far as Abraham was concerned, it was a done deal—no matter how things looked in the natural.

In fact, when you read this passage carefully, when the Bible says he did not consider his own body which was now dead, it's really saying that he did consider it, but did not allow what he saw to convince him that what God promised couldn't come to pass. That's important to understand. In all fairness to their situation at the time, Abraham and Sarah could've easily discounted God's promise and gone with what their five senses told them. If you consider their age, it's obvious that they had to walk by faith and not by sight! Abraham was almost 100 years old, and Sarah was not far behind. Now I know that in their time, in that age, many Bible scholars indicate that people aged far less rapidly than they do today, but nonetheless, you've got to really take your hat off to these two, who chose to take God's Word over what they saw and felt in the natural. If it was me in Abraham's shoes, I'm not so sure I'd be as fully "persuaded" as he was about what God had promised!

If you think it was a "slam dunk" for Abraham to ward off those thoughts about how old he and his wife were, then just head down to your local assisted-living facility and take a good look at the people living there. Ask yourself if any of those you're looking at could sire and then give birth to a baby. Yet, according to Romans, Abraham took a good look at his body, almost 100 years old, then took a good look at his wife's body, who was 90 years old, and then took a good look at God and His promise. After carefully, thoughtfully, and prayerfully considering all three, he chose to go with God's Word! Wow! When you stop to think about it, that's really impressive!

Apparently God agreed, because this is the decision that really propelled Abraham to the prominent place in Scripture that he holds for us today. Was he some kind of superman—some superhuman who was bereft of all the problems, personality quirks, and idiosyncrasies that we all deal with today? Of course not! To the contrary, Abraham was as "normal" and as subject to failure as any of us. Case in point was how he tried to pass his wife off as his sister to save his own neck in Genesis chapter 20. It wasn't exactly his most shining "faith moment," and I'm sure his wife didn't appreciate what he had done either!

You ladies that are wives out there—would you have acknowledged and appreciated the deep love of your husband if he had just tried to pawn you off as his sister to some magistrate or warlord to save his own hide? I don't think so!

But once again, we see God hard at work, calling things that be not as though they were! In this case, seeing the "father-of-our-faith" Abraham, rather than the "dump-my-wife-to-save-my-hide" Abraham! Thanks be to God, He operates by faith in all our lives! He speaks the language of Faith, which is why Abraham wasn't fried like hamburger—first by his wife and then by God! Oh, Lord, help us to do the same with God, with one another and with the situations we all face in this life.

What exactly does it mean to be "fully convinced" or "fully persuaded"? It means we're able to stand up to the lies of the devil and resist him in the Name of Jesus. It means we're able to stand up to intense public criticism—especially when it's coming from those we love, admire, or respect greatly. It means we're able to stand up for God and His Word when our declarations of Faith go against popular opinion or the majority report. It means we keep speaking the language of Faith no matter who stands against us with their words, their actions or their contempt. That's being fully persuaded, and that's how the language of Faith is used.

One of the best examples of this can be found in the Old Testament when God brings Joshua and Caleb into the Promised Land. If we start the story as recorded in Numbers chapter 13, we see that those two men were two of twelve hand-picked spies who Moses sent into the Promised Land to gather intelligence on who and what was over there. After 40 days of waiting, you can imagine how excited Moses and the Israelites were to finally see these twelve spies coming back across the Jordan River to give their Intelligence Report. However, the report itself was not what most of the Jews were ready to hear. It was a good news/bad news kind of report. At first, the report was good. It was everything they wanted to hear—a land full of lush crops and beautiful scenery, just like God had said. But then came the bad news. There were giants in the land!

> *Then they told him, and said: "We went to the land where you sent us. It truly flows with milk and honey, and this is its fruit. Nevertheless the people who dwell in the land are strong; the cities are fortified and very large; moreover we saw the descendants of Anak there. The Amalekites dwell in the land of the South; the Hittites, the Jebusites, and the Amorites dwell in the mountains; and the Canaanites dwell by the sea and along the banks of the Jordan."*
>
> —NUMBERS 13:27-29

This was bad news to almost all those who listened to the report that day. In fact, God called it a "bad report" of unbelief in Numbers 13:32. The original *King James Version* called it an "evil report" of unbelief. No matter how you look at it, they weren't speaking the language of Faith when they heard the Intelligence Report from the ten spies who walked in doubt and unbelief. Out of the twelve, only two—Joshua and Caleb—walked in faith and talked Faith to Moses and the people. Listen to Caleb as he tries to calm the people down.

> *Then Caleb quieted the people before Moses, and said, "Let us go up at once and take possession, for we are well able to overcome it."*
>
> —NUMBERS 13:30

That's the language of Faith. Yes, there are giants. Yes, they live in large, walled cities. Yes, we look like insects standing next to them. However, God said that land belongs to us, not them, so let's go up immediately and drive them out!

Caleb is calling things that be not as though they were. He's declaring the end from the beginning. He's saying that if they go up and engage the enemy, their size, fortified cities, and imposing frame will not matter. Only God's Word will matter.

But, of course, the Jews believed the majority report, and proportionately, I believe the percentages would be about the same today. If we randomly selected twelve Christians from various denominations or organizations today, put them all in a line and gave them a similar "impossible" scenario, like what those twelve spies faced when they went over and spied out the Promised Land, we'd more than likely see ten blurt out an "evil report," using the language of Doubt and Unbelief, and we'd maybe see two use the language of Faith to embrace the promises of God. And then, concerning those who heard the "report," we'd more than likely see a similar response from Christians today, much like what Moses saw that day as they heard the spies give their report. For every two who believed God and His Word, there would be about ten who didn't. And the vast majority of Christians who listened to the "facts" would do what the Jews did—begin weeping and wailing loudly, lamenting the situation and accepting defeat before the battle ever began.

Sad, isn't it? No wonder why God got angry with them back then, and why He gets angry with us today. If you continue to read through Numbers chapters 13 and 14, you can see how upset God was at how the Jews reacted to the Intelligence Report given by those ten unbelieving spies. In the end, it ultimately sealed their fate and doomed them to wander in the desert until every one of them who believed the bad report, and who were over the age of 20, died off in the wilderness. That's not what happens to those who speak the language of Faith!

What happened to Joshua and Caleb? They were protected from the judgment that came on all the unbelievers, and although they had to wander in the wilderness with the rest of them, they were divinely protected and kept alive until the time came when they could indeed enter into the Promised Land. Let's jump ahead to the book of Joshua and see what Caleb has to say to Joshua as the Promised Land is being divided up for occupation and development by the Jews.

> *"I was forty years old when Moses the servant of the LORD sent me from Kadesh Barnea to spy out the land, and I brought back word to him as it was in my heart. Nevertheless my brethren who went up with me made the heart of the people melt, but I wholly followed the LORD my God."*
>
> —JOSHUA 14:7-8

What great statements of faith we see here! What did Caleb do? He brought back word to Moses as it was in his heart. What does that mean? It means he spoke the language of Faith to Moses when he gave him his Intelligence Report after spying out the land for those 40 days. To speak the end result, you must speak as it is in your heart—not your head! Your head is where the devil will come with his thoughts, suggestions, and lies. So in order to protect your language of Faith, you must be speaking from your heart. Faith is always of the heart, not of the head. Our declarations of faith come from our inner conviction that God's Word is final authority, and as such, if the "seen" contradicts the "unseen," we go with the unseen until the seen comes into line with God's Word.

According to Caleb, the report of unbelief from the ten spies made the hearts of the people melt (as in being extremely afraid), but he wholly followed the Lord. To follow the Lord wholly is to follow Him from the heart, declaring in faith what we believe, no matter what the circumstances around us may indicate to the contrary. To follow wholly is to be single-minded on the promises of God, and that's exactly what Caleb was—single-minded and determined that what God had promised, He was able to perform, just like Abraham had been.

> *"Now therefore, give me this mountain of which the LORD spoke in that day; for you heard in that day how the Anakim were there, and that the cities were great and fortified. It may be that the LORD will be with me, and I shall be able to drive them out as the LORD said."*
>
> —JOSHUA 14:12

If you read this whole passage, you'll discover that when Caleb came to Joshua to claim his portion of the Promised Land, he was 85 years old. Not some old, slow, fragile, worn-out, sickly 85-year-old man either. In verse 11, he declares that he's "as strong this day as on the day that Moses sent me." How old was he when Moses sent him? Well, verse 10 says that God had kept him alive for the past 45 years, ever since he was sent to spy out the land, so that would mean he was 40 years old when he and the other eleven spies where sent by Moses into the Promised Land. So at the age of 85, he's still got the strength and vitality he had when he was 40 years old. That's pretty impressive, I think!

And as for this sprightly and feisty 85-year-old man, he comes along and asks Moses for the mountain. Why the mountain? Because he knows the giants live there, and he's been itching to fight them ever since he saw them 45 years earlier when he spied out the land! What an attitude! I tell you frankly, God would be embarrassed not to bless a man like this.

Notice carefully what he says to Joshua. "I shall be able to drive them out as the LORD said." Whoa! After all those years of wandering in the wilderness, watching all the unbelievers die off one by one, he still remembered what God had told him about what he could do to the giants! Think of that for a moment! Without the aid of books, CDs, online broadcasts, commentaries, Bibles, or any of the many other study tools we've got today, he was able to hold on to the promise of God for all those years! No wonder back in Numbers 14:24, God called him a man with "another spirit." What kind of "spirit"? The kind that's full of faith and knows how to speak the language of Faith.

Listen to the way Caleb talks. He's using the language of Faith. He used it back in Numbers, when he gave his report after spying out the land. He used it again in Joshua, as he comes to claim his rightful inheritance by quoting to Joshua all that God used Moses to tell him those 45 years before. I can just imagine this guy out in the wilderness, patiently waiting through more than four decades, watching the Jews perish one by one and a new generation rise up in their place. Day after day, I'm confident he'd be out there meditating on the promises of God. How else could he have remembered so well what God had said to him? No matter where they were, no matter how impossible it might have seemed, he never stopped speaking the end result. He never stopped calling those things that be not as though they were.

He did this for 45 years! Let that sink in. Not 45 minutes, hours, days, weeks, or even months. Forty-five years! Speaking Faith all those years, with no visible indication he was going anywhere except around in circles in the desert. You see, when you start talking to people about living by faith, and using the language of Faith, many times they set up "timetables" in their own mind. If God doesn't come through by a certain date, then they begin to doubt the power of faith. Ask yourself this question: Could I stand on a promise of God and wait for 45 years until it came to pass? I doubt that most of us could, including yours truly. It'd be nice to think that we could, but really, is our faith that developed? Not likely.

Why would God see fit to include such stories in the Bible for us to read? So that we could learn from them. Hebrews 6:12 tells us to imitate those who through faith and patience inherited the promises of God. Realizing that the readers of that letter where first-century Christians, you understand the only source of reference material they had to stand on would be the Old Testament scriptures. Why? Because the New Testament hadn't been written yet. It was still being written, put together. and circulated with the letters that Paul, Peter, James, and others were writing to the churches they were establishing. So when the Hebrew Christians were told to follow them, who would they be? Old Testament saints. People like Abraham and Caleb. People like David, Isaiah and others.

Go back and study carefully. Some of the greatest heroes of faith that we can read about in the Old Testament were people who, in some cases, waited decades until promises from God came to pass in their lives. And what did they do while waiting? Speak the language of Faith. Called those things that be not as though they were.

Take Noah as an example. In Genesis 7:11, it says he was 600 years old when the judgment of the flood came upon the earth. Yet it took him 120 years to build the ark before the judgment could take place.

> *And the LORD said, "My Spirit shall not strive with man forever, for he is indeed flesh; yet his days shall be one hundred and twenty years."*
>
> —GENESIS 6:3

This is when God pronounced judgment on man for his sins and wickedness. He was basically saying that on that date man was judged, but it would be 120 years before that judgment actually came to pass, which was the flood. What was Noah doing during this 120-year span of time? Building the ark! Remember, he didn't have modern tools to use like we have now. It was all by hand, and he didn't have many helpers either—just a few family members and that was it. And that ark was one big boat, dude! This was not some little bass boat he was told to build. This thing was enormous by the standards of his day, and he was told to build it by hand. So how long did Noah wait for the promise of God to come to pass? One hundred and twenty years.

And you can be sure that as he was building the ark, his neighbors had a good laugh or two at his expense! Up until then, it had never rained from the sky before. Water came up out of the ground in mist form. They had never seen lightning, thunder, rain—any of that! And what was a flood? Nobody had seen one before because it had never happened before. So here's Noah, building a boat, preparing for events that no one had ever seen before, as far as we can tell from the Scriptures. How do you stay strong during a 120-year span of time like that? By continually speaking Faith. Using the language of Faith. Calling those things that be not as though they were. I don't see how else you could do it, can you?

Then look at somebody like Moses. How long did he wait until God's promises began to come to pass in his life? Quite awhile, if you look at his life as recorded in Scripture. According to Acts 7:23-29, Moses was 40 years old when he fled into the wilderness after killing the Egyptian who was oppressing a fellow Jew. How long did Moses stay out on the back side of the desert? Acts 7:30 says it was 40 more years before he had the burning bush encounter with God. Forty years! Once again, don't read over that without taking the time to let that truth sink in. Not 40 minutes, hours, days, weeks, or months, but years. From the time he fled Egypt, 40 years passed before God called Moses to deliver the children of Israel.

God Sees Our Lives Differently Than We Do

You must understand the importance of this truth as it affects the language of Faith. God doesn't see us as we see ourselves many times. We think in terms of the culture, society, and pace of life we were born into. God thinks about us differently. We tend to see things on a day-to-day basis, while God sees our lives as a sum total of time from beginning to end. That's why it's so important to learn to speak the end result, because it might be some time before the manifestation of your Faith declaration comes to pass.

That's not an easy thing for those who are not trained to see their life through God's eyes and not their own. It takes effort to retrain our minds to think this way because most people around us, and indeed the very culture we live in, think in terms of the temporal here and now. God thinks in terms of eternity—that's the difference.

One of the best things you can do for yourself as a human being is to learn to think in terms of eternity. If we did this more consistently, we'd be much better at calling those things that be not as though they were. Speaking the language of Faith wouldn't be so hard and, seemingly, so "against the grain."

With Noah, his assignment took 120 years to complete. With Moses, he waited for 40 years on the back side of the desert before God was ready to use him. For Joshua and Caleb, they wandered with unbelieving Jews for 40 years in the wilderness, and then Caleb waited another 5 years before he presented himself to Joshua and made his request for land titles within the Promised Land. Abraham, our "father of faith," waited 25 years until the promised baby was born. That's what Hebrews 6:12 was talking about. We need to exercise faith and patience if we're to see God's promises come to pass in our lives. That's why we must read these stories from the Old Testament. God wants us to see how He sees our lives, so we'll understand the importance of speaking the end result and standing firm in faith until the manifestation comes - however long that may be.

Rule 7:
Faith Is a Language
That Is Always Positive

Jesus answered and said to him, "Blessed are you, Simon Bar-Jonah, for flesh and blood has not revealed this to you, but My Father who is in heaven. And I also say to you that you are Peter, and on this rock I will build My church, and the gates of Hades shall not prevail against it."
—MATTHEW 16:17-18

In this exchange between Jesus and Peter, we see one of Peter's more shining moments during our Lord's public ministry. After asking His disciples who men said that He was, and getting all wrong answers in reply, He specifically asked them who He was in their eyes. Never one to be timid about expressing himself, Peter jumps in and makes that classic statement about Jesus being the Christ, the Son of the Living God. This is definitely one of Peter's high water marks in his walk with the Lord. We all know about some of the silly things Peter was prone to say, but here we see this profound, sensitive, and anointed answer that is right on the money!

And Jesus is obviously impressed with Peter's answer. He immediately pronounces a blessing on him and commends Peter for being sensitive to the Holy Spirit. At that moment, I can just imagine how satisfied with himself Peter must've felt. After all, Jesus didn't talk this way about any of the other disciples, so I'm thinking he's feeling pretty good about himself right about then. But just a few verses later, as they head on down the road, Peter—the "spiritual one"—puts his foot in his mouth big time. As Jesus attempts to help them understand where He is going and what's going to happen when He gets there, Peter once again jumps in and blurts out his feelings and opinion. This time Jesus was not so impressed!

> *From that time Jesus began to show to His disciples that He must go to Jerusalem, and suffer many things from the elders and chief priests and scribes, and be killed, and be raised the third day. Then Peter took Him aside and began to rebuke Him, saying, "Far be it from You, Lord; this shall not happen to You!" But He turned and said to Peter, "Get behind Me, Satan! You are an offense to Me, for you are not mindful of the things of God, but the things of men."*
> —MATTHEW 16:21-23

Just a few minutes before, Jesus was blessing Peter and commending him for being so sensitive to the Spirit of God. And now He's calling the guy Satan! Whoa! What a difference a few verses will make! And yet, if you understand rules that govern the language of Faith, you understand that even though Peter was constantly on this "roller coaster" with the things he said and did, Jesus always made sure that, when dealing with Peter, any rebuke was ultimately balanced with as much, if not more, praise and encouragement. That's how the language of Faith operates. Faith always looks past the negative, the disappointments, the failures, and instead sees the positive, the potential, the destiny within the person—no matter what may be going on in that person's life which is contrary to God's Word and will for their life.

Another example of this, again using Peter as our subject, can be found in how Peter was specifically mentioned when the angel gave instructions as to where to meet Jesus after His resurrection.

> *But he said to them, "Do not be alarmed. You seek Jesus of Nazareth, who was crucified. He is risen! He is not here. See the place where they laid Him. But go, tell His disciples—and Peter—that He is going before you into Galilee; there you will see Him, as He said to you."*

> —MARK 16:6-7

Notice how Jesus specifically mentions Peter when using the angel to impart His instructions and directions. Why? Because Faith always sees the positive and chooses to dwell there. Faith does not dwell on the negative and doesn't waste time going back over issues, decisions, sins, and bad choices that have already been dealt with and cleansed through repentance and forgiveness. And if anyone could appreciate this rule about the Faith language, it would be Peter!

I don't think anybody could've felt worse than Peter, moments after hearing that rooster crow, after he had just finished denying Jesus for the third time in one night. The Bible says he went out and wept bitterly (Matthew 26:75). There is a difference between crying and crying bitterly. I've done them both, and I know the difference. Bitter tears are wept because the sense of grief is greater. In Peter's case, the sense of betrayal was almost more than he could bear. This horrible feeling had to be amplified by the fact that, at the Last Supper, when Jesus was trying once again to tell His disciples what was just about to happen to Him, there was Peter as usual. The first one to jump up and declare, "If I have to die with You, I will not deny You" (Mark 14:31)!

Can you imagine how terrible Peter felt when Jesus turned and looked at him after denying Him for the third time? Those "bitter tears" were well-deserved to be sure, but thank God, Jesus spoke Faith fluently, and so we see our Lord going out of His way to make sure Peter knows that His post-resurrection plans definitely include Peter! Of course, Peter needed to hear it back then, but so do we today. Human nature, if left to itself apart from being sanctified by the Word of God, will always gravitate towards the negative side of anything and anybody.

Why? Because the flesh is still dead to sin, even if our spirits are born again. And being dead to sin, our flesh always wants to see the negative because that's the sin nature in natural manifestation. The flesh can't help itself. It will gravitate towards the negative side if left unchecked. Now people may exercise some measure of discipline to control that, even apart from Christ and the New Birth, but if they at any point stop exercising the discipline and self-control, they'll find out real quick that the flesh is the flesh—alive in terms of being, but dead in terms of essence.

The Faith language goes against that bent and speaks not according to the flesh, but according to the spirit. Jesus demonstrated this throughout His public ministry when dealing with people He encountered, but especially when dealing with people like Peter. Even if Peter wept bitterly in the throes of personal anguish and despair over what he had just done in denying Jesus three times, Jesus continued to speak of him in a positive manner. Yes, I'm sure the look Jesus gave Peter was no doubt a visual rebuke (see Luke

22:61), but even so, Jesus still believed in Peter, even if Peter no longer believed in himself!

One of the Greatest Challenges

Now maybe this doesn't present such a great challenge to you, but let me tell you, this is one of the hardest language rules for me to get a handle on. Why? Because of the way I'm put together emotionally. As you know, all of us are products of a genetic mix between our mother and father. All of us have some of Mom and some of Dad in our make-up and personality. Some of us have more of Mom's personality, and some of us have more of Dad's personality. In my case, I've got much more of my father in me than my mother.

My mother was Irish through and through. She was a typical Irish redhead, full of spunk, life, and energy. My mother was always smiling, laughing, joking around, and just a pleasure to be with. She passed away not too long ago, and in memory of her, I've got a picture of her under the glass on my desk in my office. It's a picture of her with one of her trademark smiles, winking and waving her hand at the photographer, which in that case was me. I love it because, in one photo, it portrays the essence of who she was and how she lived life. She was always so effervescent, bubbly, and full of life. To this day, I so admire those qualities about her. And in part, my admiration comes from the fact that I'm not that much like her! I'm much more like my dad.

My dad was German in terms of his heritage, mannerisms, and outlook on life. By that I mean he was, for the most part, very stoic, unemotional, and analytical. He didn't smile much, at least that I can remember from growing up in our home. He just wasn't that way. In fact, I can remember one time when my younger sister came running into the room and said, "Dad's laughing—check it out!" So we all ran into the other room to see it for ourselves because it didn't happen all that much.

It's interesting to note that once, when my mother heard me say these things in a sermon somewhere, she took me to task! She wasn't upset with me, but just wanted to "set the record straight." From her perspective, her husband was very much an affectionate, emotional man. Well, maybe he was with her in private, or out in public where I might've not seen, but in the home, with us and with me in particular, he was not at all an emotional person—he just wasn't.

He was a good man, a loving father, and a capable provider for his family, but from where I stood in the home growing up, he and Mom were definitely opposites in terms of temperament and emotional makeup. You've heard the old saying that when it comes to marriage, opposites attract! Well, in my parents' case that was definitely true. My parents obviously loved each other, but they were definitely opposites! Both of them were good people. Just different.

Although my mother would disagree with me, my convictions about my dad are further reinforced by how I have turned out! In remembering both of them as I grew up at home, I know I'm much more like him than her, and as a result, it's a real challenge for me to rise above the "negative" and find the good in whatever it is I'm tempted to be negative about. This relates to just about everything in my life, from how I deal with my wife and kids, to how I mix with traffic on the freeway, to how I deal with slow checkout lines at the supermarket!

For me, it's a constant, daily challenge to stay positive. But I must do it if I'm to master the language of Faith! The language of Faith is always optimistic, never pessimistic. It always finds the good in any situation or with any person, not the bad. It's always complimentary, never critical. That's one of the rules that govern Faith because Faith is of God, and that's the way God is.

In just being the way I am because of how the genes mixed in me, by being much more like my father than my mother, I'm just inherently inclined to slide towards the negative side of life. With myself, with others, with situations I find myself in, with life in general. If I leave myself to myself, without taking the time and making the effort to renew my mind, will, and emotions to the Word of God (especially on the subject of walking in love), I will just naturally be the negative, pessimistic, sarcastic, critical kind of guy that always sees the glass half empty rather than half full.

Thank God, Jesus doesn't see us that way! Thank God, we're viewed from Heaven's perspective as successful in every way. Declared to be "more than conquerors" (Romans 8:37). Seated in heavenly places in Christ (Ephesians 2:6). Able to do all things through faith (Mark 9:23). The head and not the tail, above and not beneath (Deuteronomy 28:13). What are all these verses, and many more like them? They're expressions of Faith—part of a language that specializes in finding the good in people, not the bad. In finding the best in any situation, not the worst. I think the reason for this, more than anything else, is because of the fact that Faith works by love (Galatians 5:6), and one of the distinguishing marks of love is that it always believes the best about every person.

Love suffers long and is kind; love does not envy; love does not parade itself, is not puffed up; does not behave rudely, does not seek its own, is not provoked, thinks no evil; does not rejoice in iniquity, but rejoices in the truth; bears all things, believes all things, hopes all things, endures all things.

— 1 CORINTHIANS 13:4-7

If you look at verse 7 from the *Amplified Bible,* here's how it is translated:

Love bears up under anything and everything that comes, is ever ready to believe the best of every person, its hopes are fadeless under all circumstances and it endures everything [without weakening].

Notice that love is ever ready, or eager, to believe the best about every person. Not eager to believe the worst—but the best! That's what Faith does, because Faith is based on God's love. Faith works by love, so without love, Faith won't work. This is why many people use other rules of the language correctly and still see no tangible results in their lives. Why? Because if your walk is not the love walk, it doesn't matter what else you may know about the language of Faith. When God says that Faith works by love, He means exactly that! No love in manifestation, no effective expression of Faith. It's that simple.

Paul addressed this very issue in the first part of 1 Corinthians chapter 13, when he was teaching the Corinthians the importance of love. Here's what he said:

Though I speak with the tongues of men and of angels, but have not love, I have become sounding brass or a clanging cymbal. And though I have the gift of prophecy, and understand all mysteries and all knowledge, and though I have all faith, so that I could remove mountains, but have not love, I am nothing. And though I bestow all my goods to feed the poor, and though I give my body to be burned, but have not love, it profits me nothing.

—1 CORINTHIANS 13:1-3

Take a good look at how Paul describes the person who fails to walk in love. They have become "sounding brass" and a "clanging cymbal." That means they're nothing more than a lot of hot air! No matter what they say, their words are without substance, power, or usefulness concerning the Kingdom of God. They're just making a lot of noise that no one up in Heaven is paying any attention to.

As if that's not bad enough, God says that if you have all faith, to remove mountains if necessary, and don't walk in love, you are "nothing." Nothing! Let me tell you, when God calls you "nothing," you're in trouble! There's a whole lot of people out there in the body of Christ that think they're something, when in reality they're nothing as far as God is concerned. Why? Because they don't couple their faith walk with God's love walk. Remember the rule we're discussing here. The language of Faith is always positive, never negative. For that to become reality in our lives, we must learn how to walk in love and let God's love in us dominate.

God says that no matter what we do for Him in terms of good works and good deeds, it profits us "nothing." Once again, nothing! This means your work, your ministry, your efforts to fulfill the Great Commission and to disciple people into a closer walk with God, is of no value as far as God is concerned—until you start walking in love. Oh, yes, the people you help in ministry will definitely be blessed and ministered to, but as far as you're concerned, the work you do has no personal value and won't be rewarded when you get to Heaven someday. That's really something to think about!

How would you like to live your entire life down here on earth and then when you get to Heaven, have God describe you as a "nothing" or a "nobody," nothing more than a giant waste of time, life, and energy? Would you want to hear that? I wouldn't, and with God's help, I don't intend to. I've been in full-time ministry since 1980, and to think that if I fail to consistently walk in love, none of my work will reap me any eternal rewards! Whoa! Those are very serious consequences for choosing not to walk in love.

Is There a Beam in Your Eye?

Remember when Jesus taught about the "speck and beam" in the Gospel of Matthew? Here's what He said about how we're to relate to those around us:

> *"Judge not, that you be not judged. For with what judgment you judge, you will be judged; and with the measure you use, it will be measured back to you. And why do you look at the speck in your brother's eye, but do not consider the plank in your own eye? Or how can you say to your brother, 'Let me remove the speck from your eye'; and look, a plank is in your own eye? Hypocrite! First remove the plank from your own eye, and then you will see clearly to remove the speck from your brother's eye."*
>
> —MATTHEW 7:1-5

When I endeavor to speak Faith fluently, I must remember what Jesus taught in this passage. Faith speaks positive words and looks for the good in any and every situation. If nothing good or positive can be said, then the person fluent in Faith knows it's best to "zip the lip" and keep their mouth closed. After all, if you can't say something nice, don't say anything at all—which means that most of us would have nothing to say for days! Why? Because we're so programmed to speak in a negative vein, day in and day out.

One time the Lord challenged me to objectively analyze the words that were coming out my mouth. For a day or two, I would just concentrate on analyzing what I was saying after I said it and compare it to God's Word. I was absolutely amazed at how negative I was with my words. Towards my wife, my kids, my staff, people in general, with day-to-day situations and circumstances—everything! I was just flowing in one big, negative expression, all day long, every day.

When I realized how bad it really was, Jesus told me that Christians could put an audio recorder on their hip at the start of each day and record what they say for just one whole day. Then when they played back the tape at the end of the day they'd be shocked at what came out their mouths. Bottom line: when we compare what we're saying with God's Word about what to say and not to say, most of us fail the standard miserably. And then we wonder why the power of God is nowhere to be found when we're in some crisis, and our Faith "confessions" aren't working.

Truth be told, we have spoken in such a negative way for so long that we don't even hear ourselves when we do it. It's like when someone tells you that you said something, and you adamantly insist you never said it—until someone brings you a tape of the conversation, and lo and behold, you said it! Why didn't you hear it? Because the negative flow has become so embedded in your daily conversation and thought life, it's like "second nature" to you now.

It's like breathing air. We must, all the time, inhale and exhale air. If we stop breathing, we die. It's a part of our lives, our existence, and our very survival. Yet, we don't even think about it. We just do it. As we go about our daily affairs, we don't give breathing a second thought until something happens that impairs our ability to breathe! Then suddenly we're reminded that, whether we think about it or not, breathing is something that's going on all the time—keeping us alive day in and day out.

When Jesus instructed us not to judge lest we be judged, if you read that in context, He's basically telling us to mind our own business, instead of roaming around pointing out everyone else's faults. If we're to become fluent in Faith, we should pay no mind to what's going on in someone else's life which we may think is wrong or improper. No matter what's going on, we should be positive with the comments we make about others and just concentrate on dealing with the long list of faults we have which are still unresolved in our own lives! Trust me when I tell you, if all of us in the body of Christ did this the way He tells us to, we'd never have another disparaging word to say about anyone else—ever!

In all honesty, the issues I'm at work on in my life are more than enough to keep Jesus and myself occupied! I don't need to be pointing my finger at you or anyone else for that matter! The "beams" in my own eye are such that I don't need to be concerned about any beams, specks, particles, molecules, or atoms that may be in your eye! And if I'm to master the language of Faith, I had better walk in the light of that every day. The same holds true for you, too, and for all of us in the family of God.

The language of Faith expresses itself with compliments, not criticism. It's always eagerly looking to find the good and speak from that perspective. It's not at all like the other languages of the heart, languages expressed in the deadness of our sinful flesh. Languages like Pessimism, Cynicism, Sarcasm, and the like are the opposite of the language of Faith. Assuming a negative rumor is true before verification is a classic way these negative languages express themselves. Believing the worst will happen before it ever does is another. Hoping for failure in the lives of those we're jealous or envious of, or threatened by, is one more.

I know in my own life, as I said before, this is a constant challenge for me because of the way I'm put together emotionally. I must always take the time to renew my mind to the truths being expressed here, otherwise I immediately give the devil a place in my daily affairs. By failing to use the language of Faith and be a positive commentator on the day around me, I open my life to the whims of the enemy, and that's not a good thing to do!

Why Can't All People Drive Like Me?

As an example, when I drive I like to drive aggressively, just because of the way I approach life. I have always been one to attack—problems, challenges, traffic, everything! Very seldom do I find my peace in being passive or reactionary. It's just part of who I am, and I think that is one of the reasons why God has called me into the office of a modern-day apostle. People who stand in that particular office have to have a certain "drive" that will propel them forward in difficult or hostile circumstances or situations around the world.

Well, because of where I live and work for God, this is a constant area of renewing for me. If I'm in the Philippines, I'm continually surrounded by people who can't drive, don't want to drive, or who drive about as poorly as one could drive! Many of them never took a test to demonstrate their abilities as a driver—they just bribed someone to buy their license! And, in addition, when driving in the

Philippines, I'm also having to deal not just with bad drivers, but roads that are in terrible condition and vehicles that are old, worn out, and completely unsafe for public roads. It's life in the third world. I understand that, but if I don't renew my mind to the Word of God before I hit the road, it's going to be a challenging time for me!

When I'm in Tucson, Arizona, where we live when we're not overseas in the Philippines, I'm constantly "bombarded" with drivers who are too slow, too cautious, too old, too sick, too incoherent—whatever! And I came to the realization one day that as long as I allow the habits of other drivers to ruin my day, my day will forever be ruined because there will always be people out there who don't drive the way I think that they should!

In Tucson, as an example, during the winter months we get a lot of visitors who come down from the colder climates to winter with us in the milder temperatures of southern Arizona. That's fine, and we're all glad they become a part of our community while they wait out the harsh, cold winters back east and up north. But just as sure as I'm telling you this today, if the devil knows he can "pull my chain" or "hit my hot button" with a few drivers who might be a bit older and a bit slower, he'll have me in an emotional state of anger and stress from November to March! It'll be a never-ending parade of people on the highway who just aren't as interested as I am in driving as aggressively as I like to!

There's Bobby Boat, who is just coming back from the lake drunk, badly sunburned, and squinting because he lost his sunglasses ten minutes after he got out to the lake four days ago. Then there's Michael Motorcycle, trying to learn how to ride a motorcycle on a five-lane interstate at rush hour. Followed by Mr. Minnesota, our beloved retiree, who just flew in the day before and still has the city map draped all over the steering wheel as he cruises down that same clogged interstate at a whopping 35 miles an hour. Throw in a few Recreational Vehicles driven by people with shrunken heads who were born in the Stone Age, a couple of semi-trucks with smelly cattle on their way to the slaughter house, several landscaping crews hauling cactus away to the garbage dump, and Jed Clampett pickup trucks hauling hay to feed their horses, and you have a recipe for disaster as far as my temperament is concerned! Don't get me wrong! I love Tucson when I'm there, but honestly, I've never seen a town with more trucks in it. I think they should rename the town "Truckson" rather than Tucson. And guess what? Trucks always drive slower than I do! *Arggggghhhhh!*

Now I know that none of you ever have to deal with such things, so please indulge me, allow me to vent, and pray for me, okay? But seriously, if the devil knows he can find things like this to "rattle your chain," then, of course, he's going to do it daily—either until Jesus comes, you die from stress overload, or hopefully for God's sake and yours, you overcome these natural tendencies and start speaking the language of Faith!

Drive Thru—or Drive Over?

Ever go to the drive-thru at your local fast-food restaurant? Let me tell you if you don't already know—never use the drive-thru if you're in a hurry! This may have been a great idea 40 years ago when it was first invented, but it has now morphed into something from the pit of Hell. God only knows how many times over the years I've gotten stuck in that line while waiting for some customer ahead of me, and of course, the customer ahead of me has that "special" order that takes 25 minutes to prepare. It's the only customer all day who wants it "their way," but, of course, I'm the one who happens to pull in just seconds after they do. Sound familiar? You're in a hurry and seconds before you pull into the lane to get that "quickie meal" for on-the-go consumption, here comes the broken-down social services van full of refugees from Haiti, who haven't seen a hamburger for most of their adult lives. It's always fun to sit and wait while they attempt to decode the colorful yet disorganized and hard-to-understand menu board.

And all of that is followed by the clincher—the speaker box that makes the order-taker sound like he's in a snowstorm in the Antarctic. How I love to listen to the voice in that speaker box, with the "I-hate-this-dead-end-job" tone, as the hungry but extremely confused Haitians try to place their order. They can't understand the snowstorm voice trying to take the order, and the order-taker can't understand them because they can't speak English very well. So, of course, the order has to be placed 17 times as the order-taker tries in vain to explain what a "Happy Meal" is!

So there you are, waiting and waiting and waiting and waiting! You feel like sticking your head out the window and imploring them to order already—so you can get your food at some point before the sun goes down! By the time you get to put in your order, you're ready to order an "Unhappy Meal" with extra onions and garlic! Moments like that demand a working knowledge of the language of Faith! Positive comments, please! No mumbling, grumbling, or complaining!

My other pet nuisance is the "express" line at the local supermarket. The line that has that sign up above that clearly says you can have only nine items or less in your cart. Am I the only one who counts the number of items in the carts ahead of me? I suspect I'm not the only one! Sure enough, you're in a hurry, and to save time you enter the "express" line pushing your cart with a law-abiding nine items or less. But there in front of you is the problem! Somebody with—God forbid—10 items!

What's a Christian to do? Well, unless your mind is renewed and you're speaking the language of Faith, you might just embarrass yourself without even realizing it. "Hey, lady, lose the head of lettuce or get out of this line! Ten items! Ten items! Where's the manager? Ten items!" And then moments after you've raised your tirade about their 10 items, somebody turns to you and says, "And what do you do for a living?" So, now what? I'm sure they'd love to hear that you're a fulltime, Bible-believing, Spirit-filled, tongue-talking Christian minister! Or, you can do what I've done many times over the years in my less-than-totally-sanctified moments, which is to lie to protect your reputation! "What do I do? Well, um, I'm into sales!"

The "express" line is also the line that has the other sign that any second grader can read, which says you can pay only with cash in this line. Sorry, not with checks, credit cards, debit cards, baseball cards, gift certificates, IOUs, gold bullion recovered after World War II from sunken Japanese freighters, mutual fund redemption checks, exotic furs acquired from local Native American outlet stores, never-before-seen paintings from Picasso's "blue period" or with diamond studs recovered from the last piano Liberace played on before his death. No! No! No! Just cash! Cash! Money only, honey! Yet there they are, trying to pay with everything except cash! Positive comments, please! Positive comments!

The choice is really ours and ours alone. It takes no more effort to say something positive than it does to say something negative and critical. It's just a matter of discipline and taking the time to make this a priority in our lives. Habits can be formed either for the positive or for the negative. We decide what kind of habits control us!

I know this from personal experience. If I devote the time needed to renew my mind to the importance of being positive with my outlook on life, it has a profound effect on how I walk out each day. To the proportionate degree I do this, that's the proportionate percent of time I spend using the language of Faith in a positive presentation. On the other hand, if I let my flesh dominate and I get lazy about disciplining myself not to be negative all the time, I will gravitate back to the "old me"—a negative, complaining, grumbling, mumbling, and miserable Christian. What kind of witness is that? Not much of one as far as God is concerned!

Years ago at home growing up, my mother used to tell me that I could get more with sugar than I could with vinegar. She was a wise woman. That was true back then, and it's still true today because it's a Bible-based principle. She also taught me that laughter and the "positive approach" was always the best way to go when dealing with other people. She was living this rule and didn't even know she was! She also used to tell me that if I couldn't say something nice about somebody, I shouldn't say anything at all. There have been times in my life when I was so negative with my language, if I had tried to practice this tidbit of advice from my mother, I'd have had nothing to say for days!

So as you dedicate yourself to the task of becoming fluent in Faith, make sure you understand, appreciate, and practice the powerful principles of this particular rule. Faith is a language that speaks the positive, never the negative. Make sure you're walking in the light of this rule, or you're not going to be speaking the language of Faith!

CHAPTER FOURTEEN

Rule 8:
Faith Is a Language
of Truth

*But, speaking the truth in love, may grow up in all
things into Him who is the head—Christ.*

—EPHESIANS 4:15

Faith is a language that speaks truthfully and honestly because it works by love. No matter who likes it or not, or who is or isn't offended, Faith speaks the truth. It's a language that is completely independent of public opinion.

I heard T.L. Osborn once say that most people are slaves to the last opinion expressed about them. I believe that statement is accurate. For most of us most of the time, we live our lives according to how we think we are perceived by others or, at least, how we want them to perceive us. This is not the way of the Faith language. Faith declares the truth and is not concerned with who will like it, receive it, embrace it, or even dispute it. This is God's way, and it must become our way, too, if we're to truly become people made in His "image and likeness."

Just stop and think about it with me for a moment. How many times do you allow what others may think about you to alter what you say to them or how you say it or how much you tell them? How many times do you withhold the truth from someone simply because you're afraid of how they're going to handle it if you share it? And taking this one step further, how many times do you flat out lie to protect yourself, either in terms of saving your "reputation" or because you're afraid the other person will become mad at you? If we'd be honest with ourselves, the answer would be sobering to say the least.

The fact of the matter is this—God knows when we tell the truth and when we don't. He understands everything and knows us from the inside out. He can see into our hearts and knows the motives behind everything we think, say and do. And since we're ultimately going to stand before His judgment seat someday, it would behoove us to develop the ability and discipline of being truthful! This is what wisdom is all about.

Wisdom Is Knowing How to Use Your Mouth Correctly

If you study the book of Proverbs, you will learn God's definition of wisdom. Proverbs is full of verses talking about the tongue, words, and verbal communication. Proverbs teaches us that if we walk in godly wisdom, we'll always know what to say, what not to say; how to say it and how not to say it; when to say it and when not to say it; and who to say it to and who not to say it to.

In Ecclesiastes 3:1-8, God talks extensively about the importance of recognizing the right time for things we think, say, or do. In verse 7, He tells us there's a time to speak and a time to keep silent. How important it is to know the difference! When we walk in God's wisdom, we always have the right sense of timing. We know, because we're in touch with God's Spirit within, when to speak and when to hold back. But even when we know in our hearts it's better to keep quiet, understand that sooner or later, God will maneuver us into a position when it will be the right time to speak the truth in love!

In addition to these truths, we must also remember that at no time in the Word does God ever instruct us to lie or be verbally evasive with the people in our lives who need the truth. We are to know how to speak properly and when to speak properly, and as far as God is concerned, that includes knowing the importance of being honest and truthful with those we're speaking to—whenever it's our time to declare the truth in love.

The best example of this is Jesus. Go back and read the four Gospels carefully. Read the verbal exchanges He had with God, with His disciples, with the common people He was trying to minister to, with His religious enemies, and, finally, with the devil himself. Frankly, in most of our circles of "fellowship" which we have today, if we were half as honest and blunt as He was in His day in His circles of fellowship, we'd be branded as being cold, callous, insensitive, abrasive, and unnecessarily confrontational. It's interesting to note that for the most part, Christians today agree that Jesus was a "loving" man and knew how to "walk in love." Yet if we ever dare speak as honestly as He did to these same people, we would immediately be accused of not walking in love! The hypocrisy is glaring.

I've learned this truth personally in ministry. As a minister of the Gospel, I often find myself in counsel with folks who supposedly want me to tell them what I think they should do in whatever situation they may be in. But what

I've found out is this: when most people ask you for your opinion or counsel as a minister, what they're really asking for is your approval about a decision they've already made or an opinion they've already embraced. They aren't really interested in what you think—if what you think differs with what they want to hear. Now there are some exceptions to this, but by and large, this is the way it is for most people who come along and want to "counsel" with you.

And God forbid if you actually speak the truth to them! Do they thank you for it? Do they shake your hand and express their gratitude for having someone care enough to tell them the truth? Do they go out, prayerfully consider the truthful things you said, and implement changes accordingly? No, that's not the case most of the time! Most of the time, the reaction will be similar to the kind of reaction Jesus got when He spoke the truth to those around Him. People will get mad at you. They'll be offended with you. They'll tell others that you're not walking in love. They'll leave your church. They'll refuse to fellowship with you anymore. They'll look the other way when they see you coming towards them. They'll ask to be removed from your mailing list. Why? All because you spoke truth into their lives which went contrary to what they wanted to hear!

I remember one example of this in my own ministry. I once was good friends with a man who walked with a heavy anointing in the office of the evangelist. When this man operated in his God-given office, and flowed in the Holy Spirit, he was one of the most anointed ministers I've ever seen. People would get saved, sick folks would get healed, and several of the nine gifts of the Spirit would manifest through him accurately and often. The trouble was he was trying to pastor a local church at the time, and he was losing members.

He came to me one day and asked me for my advice. In essence, he asked me if I knew why he was losing his members. When this church was at its peak, it numbered well over 300, if you included the youth and the children. But when he came to me to ask for my opinion, the church had dwindled down to about 30 members, and if something wasn't done to reverse the tide, he'd eventually have to close the church down. So he came to me and wanted my counsel about why this had happened and what could be done to remedy the problem.

I asked him, "You really want to know what the problem is?"

"Oh, yes, Mike, please, tell me the truth. I need to know what's wrong here."

I said, "Okay, but remember, you asked me. I didn't come to you. You came to me." I said to him, "The problem with this church is you're not a pastor. You're an evangelist trying to pastor, and that's why you're driving all the sheep away."

You see, if you would ever sit under this man's ministry and listen to him preach, you could easily see he was not a pastor, but an evangelist. His style of delivery, his mannerisms, the way he interpreted Scriptures and put messages together—all of it was done and said as an evangelist, not as a pastor. And that's fine because that's what he was called and anointed to be, but not as the pastor of a local church body. He would "scream" his message at the people each weekend, and that's not what people need to hear from their shepherd. They need to be cared for, as a pastor is called to care for the sheep. They don't need to get saved all over again every weekend, and they don't need someone preaching to them with that "angry look" that many times will accompany the fervor of an evangelistic message.

If you've ever been to a meeting and listened to a true evangelist, you understand what I mean when I refer to the "angry look"! I had that "look" in the early days of my own ministry, when God used me mostly in the office of an evangelist. But later, when the apostolic office came upon me, much of my delivery style changed. If you go back and listen to my messages from the early years of my ministry, and listen to my messages today, you'd instantly recognize a distinct difference in many areas of my delivery. The truth contained in the messages remains the same, but the delivery is apostolic now, rather than evangelistic. There is a difference.

Honestly, if I was a member going to that man's church, and had to listen to him preach his evangelistic messages every Sunday, I'd have left too! But, to make the long story short, when I told him these things he got offended at me and hasn't spoken to me since, and this incident happened many years ago. We were good friends, and had done many ministry outreaches together, but when I told him the truth he got mad at me. Why? Because it didn't agree with what he wanted to hear. He wanted someone to come along and take his side and say that all the people who had left were wrong. If I had told him that, it would've made him feel good, and probably we'd still be good friends to this day, but I couldn't say that because it wasn't the truth.

A good friendship ended that day, simply because I spoke the truth in love, as the Word tells us to do in Ephesians 4:15. When you speak the language of Faith, be prepared for things like this to happen. They will. They happened to Jesus frequently, and they'll happen to you too. There are some people who just can't handle the truth, and when it's spoken to them they're going to get mad at you. You can't help it, and you can't avoid it. All you can do is tell the truth, and remember that you're doing it as unto the Lord, not for public approval or acceptance.

Again, go back and look at how Jesus spoke the truth with people. Remember when He was in the temple speaking to the religious leaders of His day? Here's His warm, fuzzy declaration:

> *"Woe to you, scribes and Pharisees, hypocrites! For you travel land and sea to win one proselyte, and when he is won, you make him twice as much a son of hell as yourselves."*
>
> —MATTHEW 23:15

Wow! Isn't that an uplifting statement? I can just see the Pharisees, Sadducees, and scribes sitting there, and upon hearing that, they turn to one another and say, "Isn't that good? I'm so blessed! I'm so comforted! I'm so edified!" How would people react or respond today if some preacher did that in church during a Sunday service?

You know how we preachers like to have the congregation turn to one another and speak some statement of truth which helps us amplify the point we're trying to make in our sermons? The preacher will say to the congregation, "Turn to your neighbor and tell him that God loves him!" Have you ever had preachers do that with you? I've done it, and I've heard many others do it too. Can you just imagine Jesus telling the temple crowd that day, "Now turn to your neighbor and say, 'You're twice as much a child of Hell as I am!'" Whoa! That would be a moment not soon forgotten in that meeting!

Or how about Jesus talking to the Jews in the eighth chapter of John? Look at this soft, comforting, gentle, and soothing statement:

> *"Yet you have not known Him, but I know Him. And if I say, 'I do not know Him;' I shall be a liar like you."*
>
> —JOHN 8:55

Yeah! Praise God, Mike, what a warm, uplifting declaration! Jesus called His audience liars to their faces! But wait, earlier in the sermon, He nailed them again with this marvelous passage of love:

> *"Why do you not understand My speech? Because you are not able to listen to My word. You are of your father the devil, and the desires of your father you want to do. He was a murderer from the beginning, and does not stand in the truth, because there is no truth in him. When he speaks a lie, he speaks from his own resources, for he is a liar and the father of it. But because I tell the truth, you do not believe Me."*

—JOHN 8:43-45

Notice carefully that Jesus is speaking the truth. He says so several times, especially in the passage we're looking at from John's Gospel. And how do you think His truthful statements were received? With gratitude? With relief that somebody had finally come along to love them honestly enough to tell them the truth? No! Sermons like this were what we like to call the "straw that broke the camel's back." The religious leaders had been putting up with Jesus for almost three years—getting upset with Him, mocking Him, criticizing Him, resisting Him—but these messages, delivered in the temple, right in their own "backyard," so to speak, were just too much for them to handle. Just a few days later they arrested Him and murdered Him.

Hmmmmmm. So we see that in these passages, our Lord Jesus, the epitome of what it means to walk in love, is calling the religious leaders of His day liars and children of Hell—to their faces! If you did that today, publicly, in some-body's service or church, how do you think that would go over? You can answer that one for yourself because you already know what the reaction would be.

And then there were those other marvelous adjectives Jesus used to describe the Pharisees, Sadducees, and scribes. Shall I give you a few of them? He called them:

Whited sepulchers (Matthew 23:27).

Full of dead men's bones (Matthew 23:27).

Children of hell (Matthew 23:15).

Liars (John 8:55).

Imitators of their father the devil (John 8:44).

Blind men who say they can see (John 9:41).

Blind leaders of the blind (Matthew 15:14).

Sons of murderers who killed God's prophets (Matthew 23:29-31).

Hypocrites (Matthew 15:7 and many other places as well).

Did these people "receive Him"? Let's just put it this way. After Jesus got done with His sermons and sat down, I don't think these people ran to the synagogue lobby to sign up on His mailing list. I don't think they bought all His books and CDs. No, the Bible says they went out and plotted how they might put Him to death. That's not exactly a "positive response"!

So when you dedicate yourself to learning the language of Faith, understand Rule 8. The Faith language speaks the truth in love. Period. No excuses. No apologies. No retractions. We say it and leave it there. We declare the truth and let those we declare it to receive it or reject it. We're not swayed by public opinion or response, and we certainly are not manipulated by whether or not we're being "received" by those we're speaking to. The language of Faith goes way above and beyond that shallow kind of mentality.

When you speak the language of Faith, you'll be maligned, ridiculed, vilified, gossiped about, lied about, and laughed at. They laughed at Jesus when He came to the dead girl's house in Mark 5:40 and declared to them the truth. So don't be surprised if they do it to you too! Don't run from it when it happens, but rather, embrace it and allow the experience to stiffen your resolve in this matter. Truth is truth, and nothing changes that! The language of Faith speaks truth. Honesty, forthrightness, directness, boldness, independence—all these adjectives describe the man or woman using the language of Faith. Do they describe you?

CHAPTER FIFTEEN

Rule 9:
Faith Is a Language
That Demands
Discipline

So then, my beloved brethren, let every man be swift to hear, slow to speak, slow to wrath.

—JAMES 1:19

Think about what this verse is saying. When James says that every man needs to do this, he's talking about you and me—all of us inside the body of Christ. Three things are mentioned. First, we're to be swift to hear. Second, we're to be slow to speak. Third, we're to be slow to wrath. Swift to do one thing, slow to do two things. Swift to hear, or in other words, to be more inclined to listen than anything else. We're also told to be slow to wrath, which means that we're to manage our emotions and not let anger usurp authority in our lives. And we're also told to be slow to speak, and that's the part we're especially interested in here.

As Kenneth Hagin once said in one of his books, most Christians practice this verse in reverse. Most believers are slow to listen, swift to speak, and swift to get angry. That's tragic, because if we don't get control of our mouths, we'll never become fluent in the language of Faith. As we've already established, all language is comprised of words, and to learn any language, you must learn the words of the language and the rules that govern the usage of those words. Then you can arrange and use those words to express yourself to others who know that particular language. When speaking Faith, verbal discipline is essential; otherwise, we'll be unable to use Faith to tap into all the power that's reserved for those who know how to speak the language.

Let me say it this way. To speak Faith, we must be disciplined to think before we speak. We must be people who are "slow to speak," publicly as well as privately. We must be people who learn the value of listening before speaking, and the value of thinking before speaking, and the importance of weighing the words we're about to speak before speaking them.

Private Conversation Is Where It All Begins

The longer I live my life in Christ, the more I see the importance of learning to manage my mouth in private. The problems most of us have with uncontrolled conversation in public can be traced back to a lack of discipline with our mouths privately. If we can't manage our mouths in private, when no one is around to hear us but God, we're certainly not going to be able to do it publicly when others are listening to what we're saying. Private management of our conversation is where we begin the quest to master our mouths, because if we don't control our mouths, we'll never be able to control the rest of the flesh, and that's something all of us need to remember.

> *For we all stumble in many things. If anyone does not stumble in word, he is a perfect man, able also to bridle the whole body.*

—JAMES 3:2

What a statement! This is truly one of those all-encompassing statements too important to ignore. Through James, the Holy Spirit is telling us that if we're going to ever get control over our dead-to-sin flesh, we must first get control over our mouths. Why? Because if we can't get control of our tongues, we'll never be able to control our flesh. That is significant!

Do we really understand this? When we endeavor to learn the language of Faith, we must realize that our ability to use Faith is largely determined by the degree of discipline we exert over our flesh, and whatever problems we may have with our flesh can be traced back to our failure to control our tongues! On the other hand, to the degree we're able to control the mouth, that's the proportionate degree we're able to control the flesh!

And where do we begin this disciplinary process? With our private conversations. It's important to master our mouths in private, because that's the first step towards mastering our mouths in public, which takes us to the point in our lives where we really and truly control our flesh and keep it under concerning our born-again spirit's desire to obey God and do His will.

What do I mean when I refer to "private conversation"? I mean the conversations, comments, observations, and statements made in any setting or environment where we, as the speakers, say things we would otherwise not want repeated in public. It could be things we say to ourselves while we're alone, or it could be things we say amongst a group of other people. Either way, our private conversations are those we speak only because we think nobody else besides ourselves, or outside our little group, is going to hear what we're saying. Unfortunately for those who think their conversations are indeed private, God tells us something completely different. Look at what He says to the Jews:

> *"Nevertheless you would not go up, but rebelled against the command of the LORD your God; and you complained in your tents, and said, 'Because the LORD hates us, He has brought us out of the land of Egypt to deliver us into the hand of the Amorites, to destroy us.'"*
>
> —DEUTERONOMY 1:26-27

If you read the verses surrounding the two we've quoted here, you'll see that God is using Moses to remind the Jews about the penalties of unbelief, penalties that their forefathers had to pay because of their lack of faith. And how did much of that lack of faith manifest? Through their mumbling, grumbling, and complaining against God and His servant Moses. And where was much of this complaining taking place? In their tents!

In other words, their complaining was being done in private, where the complainers thought they were alone, where nobody else would hear what they were saying. How wrong they were! It would seem that according to this passage, small groups of Jews would get together in their tents and have a private "Let's bash Moses" party. It could've been husbands and wives mumbling to each other as they lay down before sleep, or it could've been groups that included neighbors, friends, or other family members. Either way, what we see here are people who appear to be loyal and supportive in public, but when the tent flaps are closed, privately criticize the leadership of Moses and openly question God's power and ability to lead them to the land of milk and honey.

> *Then they despised the pleasant land; they did not believe His word, but complained in their tents, and did not heed the voice of the LORD.*
>
> —PSALM 106:24-25

This accounts of what we just looked at in Deuteronomy and Psalms specifically tell us that not only did the children of Israel complain privately in their tents, but they did not listen to God and disobeyed His directions and commands. Friend, God hears every word we speak, wherever we speak it. More than that, He understands and sees into our hearts, knowing not just what we're saying, but why we're saying it. And as we'll see in other verses we look at here, God keeps records of everything we say and will bring those words forth for judgment on the day we stand before Christ at His judgment seat.

Before we master the language of Faith, we must think before we speak, especially when speaking privately. If we don't, we take ourselves out of faith to the proportionate degree we engage in unscriptural conversation, which no one else might ever hear, but which God hears loud and clear. The Jews were guilty of doing this, and God took them to task over it. He didn't like it at all, and those Jews who did it paid the penalty for it. Those private conversations inside their tents, whether alone or in small groups of friends or family, were the words that undid their faith and took them out of position to receive God's power, provision, and protection. We need to learn from their mistakes.

Nor complain, as some of them also complained, and were destroyed by the destroyer.

—1 CORINTHIANS 10:10

If you read this verse in context, you'll see it's there to show us how the Jews got into sin with their words and actions back in the Old Testament. How did the destroyer get in to steal, kill, and destroy against the Jews? According to this verse, his opening was created when the Jews began to murmur and complain against Moses and, ultimately, against God. And where was all this murmuring and complaining being done? Mostly in their tents! To be sure, there were times in public when people questioned the leadership of Moses, but rest assured, for every public confrontation that took place, there were many more private instances where those Jews were getting to trash-talk against Moses.

We must be "slow to speak" in our tents, which for us today would be the equivalent of private conversation in our home with family or friends or in the bedroom with our spouse or in the car while driving or wherever we retreat for privacy and seclusion. And as I said, private conversations could be words we blurt out while being completely alone or with small groups of friends or family in secluded and private settings, away from the public arena.

God Has A Book of Remembrance

Remember, I told you that God keeps a record of every word we've ever spoken. In Matthew 12:36, Jesus said that every idle word men speak will be judged in the day of judgment. In 1 Samuel 3:19, God told Samuel that He would not let a single one of his words fall to the ground. And then in Malachi, God specifically tells us about a book

He calls the Book of Remembrance. Here's what He says about it:

> *"Your words have been harsh against Me,"* says the Lord, *"Yet you say, 'What have we spoken against You?' You have said, 'It is useless to serve God; what profit is it that we have kept His ordinance, and that we have walked as mourners before the Lord of hosts? So now we call the proud blessed, for those who do wickedness are raised up; they even tempt God and go free.'"*
>
> *Then those who feared the Lord spoke to one another, and the Lord listened and heard them; so a book of remembrance was written before Him for those who fear the Lord and who meditate on His name. "They shall be Mine,"* says the Lord of hosts, *"on the day that I make them My jewels. And I will spare them as a man spares his own son who serves him." Then you shall again discern between the righteous and the wicked, between one who serves God and one who does not serve Him.*
>
> —MALACHI 3:13-18

What a great and, at the same time, revealing passage here in Malachi! There are so many nuggets of truth here, we could camp on this passage for weeks. But for the purposes of this book, let's focus our attention on this "Book of Remembrance" that God talks about.

First of all, notice that in verse 13, God tells the Jews that their words have been harsh against Him. What do "harsh" words against God mean as far as He's concerned? Complaining. Mumbling. Murmuring. Grumbling. With a tone of contempt and bitterness in the words spoken. Harsh words are not just the words themselves, but the attitude behind the words being spoken. These people were getting into their tents and privately bashing God over issues they didn't like about what they thought God should be doing on their behalf.

It's important to read these verses in context, because just in front of this passage we find those classic verses we use so much when it comes time to take up church offerings or teach on tithing. Let's remember that the book of Malachi, as well as all the books of the Bible, were not originally written in chapter and verse format. When first penned by the hand of Malachi, this letter was one long book, with no verse markings and no chapter headings.

When God talks to them about the importance of tithing to prove His faithfulness over financial blessings, we find right after those statements that God begins to chastise the Jews for the murmuring they've got going against Him in these areas of financial supply and surplus. Notice also that when God calls their attention to what they've been saying against Him, they don't even realize they've been doing it! When God tells them that their words have been harsh against Him, they immediately reply incredulously and say, "When have we ever spoken harshly against You?" Obviously, they don't even know what they've been doing to cut God off and prevent Him from blessing them the way they're expecting to be blessed.

So it is today in many of our churches, homes, marriages, and family relationships. With the help of the devil, of course, we get ourselves into a negative flow of conversation, and without even realizing what we've done, we've opened the door to the devil and allowed him to come in and rob us and, at the same time, prevent God from moving on our behalf. And although this passage, in context, specifically refers to the degree of financial blessings we can or cannot receive from God, the principle here transcends every other area of our lives as well. It applies to our ministries, our jobs, and our careers, our families and our marriages, and in how we work with and relate to other members of the body of Christ, wherever and whenever they're introduced into our lives.

Some of this is done publicly, of course, but the real damage is done when we have an undisciplined tongue in private—when we think the general public won't find out what we're saying in secret. That is where we must look first and where we need God's help to shore up openings in our armor which we've given to the devil.

In verse 14 of this passage in Malachi, God recounts specifically what these complainers have been speaking harshly against Him. He tells them that, basically, they've been comparing what they've got in return for serving God to what the wicked have as they continue to ignore God and live for themselves. That's not a good thing to do, my friend! They're complaining amongst themselves, asking themselves what the value is in continuing to serve God and keep His commandments—with very little to show for it—while the ungodly are off doing their own thing and living lives of opulence and ease.

But then beginning in verse 16, God starts talking about the ones who are not complaining and mumbling against Him. He tells us that they're gathering together, too, just like the complainers, but not for the same purposes. Instead of gathering together privately to secretly bash God and speak harshly against Him, these other Jews are gathering together to honor Him, praise Him and show the respect due His Holy Name. That's what it means when it says they were "fearing the Lord." What did God do for those whose conversations reflected their fear, honor and respect for Him? He put all their words in His Book of Remembrance!

Verses 17 and 18 tell us that God is going to reward those who resist the temptation to speak harshly against

God. He is going to bless them, exalt them, promote them, and give them prominent places of leadership and authority. They will be spared the judgment that is coming against those who speak against Him, and they will be blessed with the discernment from Heaven to judge between the righteous and wicked. Who are the righteous and who are the wicked in this passage? According to verse 18, the wicked are the people of God who speak harshly against Him, and the righteous are the people of God who bless God with their words—words which are recorded in His Book of Remembrance.

Please note that according to this passage in Malachi, the Book of Remembrance seems to be reserved only for the words spoken by God's people which please Him and demonstrate faith and fear towards His Name. However, keep in mind that whatever words come out our mouths, they will be remembered and judged at Christ's judgment seat unless we repent and ask forgiveness from the Lord beforehand. That fact alone should be incentive enough for us to take a hard, objective look at the words coming out our mouths and, if necessary (and it probably will be), become radical in changing the pattern of conversation we engage in day in and day out.

Paul said it this way to the Philippian church:

> *Therefore, my beloved, as you have always obeyed, not as in my presence only, but now much more in my absence, work out your own salvation with fear and trembling; for it is God who works in you both to will and to do for His good pleasure.*
>
> *Do all things without complaining and disputing, that you may become blameless and harmless, children of God without fault in the midst of a crooked and perverse generation, among whom you shine as lights in the world,*

holding fast the word of life, so that I may rejoice in the day of Christ that I have not run in vain or labored in vain.
                                        —PHILIPPIANS 2:12-16

It's impossible to be blameless, harmless, and without rebuke in this twisted and perverse world until we get control of our tongues, stop mumbling against God in private, and become fluent in Faith. Verse 14 sums it all up—do all things without murmuring and disputing. The last time I checked the English language dictionary, the word "all" means all! It doesn't mean "most." It doesn't mean "some." It doesn't mean "almost all." It doesn't mean "a few." It means exactly what it means—all!

So what does this mean for us as believers today? It means that the moment words come out our mouths which God considers to be murmuring, complaining, or mumbling words against Him and His Word, we're in disobedience to God and guilty of violating the Scriptures. In case you weren't aware, that's called sin as far as God is concerned! May God help us all!

It Takes Intense Discipline to Master the Mouth

Do you remember the rule we're discussing here in this chapter? In order to speak the language of Faith fluently, we must exercise the discipline required to get control of our tongues and keep control of our tongues for the rest of our lives. As you've probably discovered, like I have, this is no easy task. It demands hard work and daily dedication to the goal in front of us. Our tongue, according to James chapter 3, is an unruly evil, full of deadly poison. When undisciplined, it becomes the kindling Satan uses to set our lives on fire and destroy everything God has done, is doing or is trying to do in our lives for His glory and our well-being. James says it this way:

> *Indeed, we put bits in horses' mouths that they may obey us, and we turn their whole body. Look also at ships: although they are so large and are driven by fierce winds, they are turned by a very small rudder wherever the pilot desires. Even so the tongue is a little member and boasts great things.*
>
> *See how great a forest a little fire kindles! And the tongue is a fire, a world of iniquity. The tongue is so set among our members that it defiles the whole body, and sets on fire the course of nature; and it is set on fire by hell.*
>
> —JAMES 3:3-6

The tongue is the avenue which gives God opportunity to bless us—or which gives the devil opportunity to destroy us. Notice that in verse 6, the tongue is called that which defiles the whole body and sets on fire the course of nature. This is why it's so important to practice speaking Faith and to learn the rules which govern the usage of that language. This particular rule is one which cannot be over-looked, because in our day and age, everybody wants something for nothing. Or, they want something of value without putting in the hard work required to get it. We, in our modern society, have developed the "microwave mentality." We want, and expect, everything to be done quickly, with as little discomfort and effort as possible.

God doesn't work that way. He never has, and He never will. He's not obligated to jump when we want Him to jump, and He's certainly not required to adapt His operation to our "instant everything" type of mentality. On the other hand, He has put in place a spiritual system of communication which, when adhered to, creates an unlimited pipeline of blessings, power, provision, guidance, and protection—from the day we are born again until the day we exit planet Earth. It's called the language of Faith!

That's why discipline is so essential to the mastering of this language. The world system all around us is developed and controlled by Satan. There are multitudes of evil spirits roaming to and fro on assignment, attempting to do their level best to torment us, hinder us, hurt us, and, if possible, kill us before our time. We live in a physical body that is still dead to sin, which has no desire to live for God in any way. We must do what Paul told the Corinthians in 1 Corinthians 9:27. We must "keep the body under," and let me tell you that is a fulltime job! The work of disciplining our tongues goes on and on—every day of our lives. Just because we've mastered the Faith language yesterday does not guarantee we'll have it mastered today—or tomorrow for that matter. We have to develop the disciplines needed every day to keep the body under, force it to obey God's Word, and exert the strength needed to successfully ward off the demons and the world system they're operating against us.

No, it's not easy, but it's necessary, so let's quit looking for lame excuses to justify our ineptness and failures and get busy becoming the lean, mean, fighting machines God has ordained us to be in Christ! As I've said before, nobody learns to speak new languages fluently by accident. They master new languages by dedicating themselves to the disciplines necessary to make the mastery possible. It doesn't just happen. They create the environment to make it happen. The same is true for learning the language of Faith. If you're not willing to put in the time, energy, and effort to discipline your dead flesh, you can forget about ever becoming fluent in Faith.

Sometimes Movies Can Be A Blessing

There's a movie which came out in 2004 called "Miracle." It's produced by Walt Disney Films, and it's based on the true story about how the USA amateur men's hockey team won the gold medal in the 1980 Winter Olympics in Lake Placid, New York. When it was playing in theaters, I went several times to see it, and when it came out on DVD I bought it right away. As you watch this movie, there are so many spiritual applications one can draw from listening to the dialogue between the team's coach and his players.

To give you a broad overview of the movie, the Soviet men's hockey team had dominated world hockey since 1960, which was the last time the USA had won a medal in Olympic hockey competition. Since that particular Olympiad, the Soviet hockey team had won the gold medal in every succeeding Olympics and had never been beaten in Olympic competition by anyone, anywhere. Over the same span of time, the USA amateur men's hockey program had become pretty much a laughingstock at the world-class level of play.

Less than one year before the 1980 Winter Olympics were to begin in Lake Placid, the USA Olympic hockey officials hired a man named Herb Brooks to assemble, train, and coach the hockey team that would represent the USA in the upcoming Olympics. Coach Brooks had successfully coached at the university level, but this was the Olympics, and his job was daunting to say the least. He was hired to pick, train, coach, and mold a team of immature, selfish, ego-centered college kids into a team that would be able to competitively skate with teams like that of the Soviet Union—teams that had skated together for many years, won many championships, and dominated the sport of hockey in convincing and intimidating fashion at the world-class level.

As the movie unfolds, we see Coach Brooks begin to apply his philosophies and techniques to first pick his team and then to train and prepare his team. Now, whether or not every line in the movie is an actual quote from Coach Brooks is something you and I as the viewer may never know, but nonetheless, the storylines, as presented during the course of the movie, reflect the intensity and discipline that was required of these players to raise their game to a level they had never gone to before.

On the night they were to compete against the Soviets for the right to play for the gold medal, after they had already beaten almost every other team that used to beat our teams consistently, Coach Brooks gives his locker-room pep talk. One point he emphasized really stuck out to me as I watched the movie. He said to his players, in essence: Boys, whether we win or lose, we're going to skate with the Soviets for all three periods of play. No team has ever been able to match their level of conditioning and intensity for three periods of play, but we will *because we can*! We will shut them down *because we can*! We will compete at their level *because we can*!

Oh, my, when he said those things to his players my spirit jumped within me! What a powerful truth! The players on that USA Olympic hockey team weren't as good individually as their Soviet counterparts, but the reason Coach Brooks said they could beat them was because, through intense disciplines and hard training, they had raised their game to the same level as that of the Soviets. Because of the disciplines they had applied to themselves, they had put themselves in a position to win. It was now possible!

Well, if you know sports history, you know the USA hockey team went out that night and shocked the entire world by beating the Soviets 4-3. The Soviet hockey team had not been defeated in 20 years of Olympic play, but this former ragtag bunch of American college hockey players did the impossible because they were willing to exercise the discipline necessary to put themselves in position to win.

We can do the same for ourselves when it comes to Faith and the disciplining of our tongue. It's not up to God, my friend. It's up to us. God has given us every gift, every blessing, every promise necessary to get the job done in grand and glorious fashion. We've been commissioned to go into all the world and preach the Gospel to every creature, and it will take great faith and a very trained tongue to do that. Satan will stand against us every step of the way, but just like how the USA hockey team defeated the Soviets back in the 1980 Winter Olympics and ulti- mately won the gold medal, so we can master Faith and push back the forces of darkness wherever God sends us by His Spirit. We will take territory for God because we can! We will overcome personal obstacles and hurdles because we can! We can do it. Philippians 4:13 says we can do all things through Christ who strengthens us. How? With Faith! Using the language of Faith! By exercising the disci- plines necessary to keep our tongues in submission to our spirits and to God's Word.

The devil will fight you every step of the way. The world system will laugh at you and try to get you to go back to its way of negative communication. Our flesh will contest every decision we make to discipline the flesh. It won't be easy, but then again nothing is when the rewards are so great and our potential so huge in Christ. The reason our enemies will rise up and try their best to hinder us is because they know how powerful we'll be in Christ with a disciplined, godly tongue.

Maybe you've tried a thousand times to get control of your tongue, and each time it seemed like the devil, his world system, and your flesh just swallowed you up and spit you out in utter contempt. That's the past. Today is a new day, so seize it with God's help, and with your decision to dedicate yourself to this task 100 percent, expect things to change!

Speak by faith! Use the language of Faith and begin calling those things that be not as though they were, as Abraham did in Romans 4:17-22. Say it out loud! Let yourself hear yourself! Boldly declare that, according to Psalm 45:1, your mouth is the pen of a ready writer, and God is your writer bringing His perfect will to pass in your life! Praise God! As you begin doing this, you'll be amazed at how your tongue begins to come into line with God and His Word. You'll be slow to speak, thinking before speaking, and no matter where you are or what circumstances you're in, you'll speak words that continually keep you connected with Heaven's blessings, power, protection, and provision. You'll become fluent in Faith!

It's time to start!

PRAYER OF SALVATION

If you've never received Jesus as Lord and Savior, you can do that right now, wherever you are—and you don't need anyone with you to do this. Even if you're by yourself, you can pray the prayer below from your heart, out loud to the Lord, and receive the free gift of eternal salvation. Jesus stands at the door to every man's heart and knocks, but only we can open the door (Rev. 3:20). The Bible says with the heart we believe and with the mouth we confess our salvation (Rom. 10:9,10). Right now, therefore, lift your heart and voice to the Lord and pray this prayer:

Dear Lord Jesus, I believe that You are the Son of God and that You died on a cross, paid for my sins, and rose from the dead. Therefore, right now, I open the door to my heart, and I choose to make You the Lord of my life. I confess You as my Lord and personal Savior, and I ask You to come into my heart now. I repent of all my sins, receive my forgiveness, and accept You as the Lord and Savior of my life—for the rest of my life. From this day forward, I will live for You and You alone, my Lord Jesus. Thank You, Lord, for loving me and for saving my soul. Amen.

If you prayed that simple prayer sincerely from the heart, the Lord has heard you and done exactly what you have asked. The Holy Spirit has come and recreated your spirit man on the inside, and you are now a born-again child of God (John 3:3). This is the greatest miracle anyone can receive, and it happened because of your faith! You're saved now, not because of how you feel after you prayed but because of the choice you made before you prayed! You made a decision, and your salvation is based upon that decision. You reached out and chose to receive the free gift of salvation by making Jesus Lord of your life (John 1:12; Rom. 5:17). Congratulations!

Please contact me, and share the good news about your decision today to make Jesus the Lord of your life. All of heaven rejoices with you and for you (Matt. 18:12-14), and I'm so very proud of you!

REVEREND MIKE KEYES, SR.

ABOUT THE AUTHOR

Mike Keyes grew up in Ohio and was raised in the Roman Catholic church. In 1973, he graduated from college to become a successful advertising executive and graphic artist. On September 21, 1978, at age twenty-six, he was born again and Spirit filled two days later. Immediately, the gifts of the Spirit began working in his life. Through his local church, he began to witness on the streets, in area prisons, and anywhere he could hand out tracts.

In September 1979, Reverend Keyes resigned his job to attend Rhema Bible Training Center in Tulsa, Oklahoma, graduating in May 1980. In September 1980, he traveled to the Philippines with a one-way plane ticket, arriving without knowledge of the language or customs and with no one there to meet him. When he got off that plane to begin his ministry, he had twenty dollars in his pocket, one footlocker containing his Bible, class notes, a few changes of clothing, and the promise of support totaling $250 from no one except his parents and one small church in Toledo, Ohio.

From those humble beginnings and through his faithfulness to the calling of God over the years, the Lord has used Reverend Keyes extensively to reach untold numbers of people in the Philippines and around the world. Always emphasizing outreach to the remote, overlooked, out-of-the-way villages and towns that no one else has gone to, it is conservatively estimated that since the beginning of his ministry's outreach in 1980, over 750,000 souls have been won to Christ in his nationwide crusades in the Philippines.

Mike Keyes Ministries International (MKMI) is an apostolic ministry that reaches the lost, teaches the Christians and trains the ministers. With a consistent crusade outreach, a church network of hundreds of churches, and the Rhema Bible Training Center, Reverend Keyes and his staff, pastors, graduates and students continue to fulfill the Great Commission wherever he is instructed to go by the Holy Spirit—throughout the Philippines and around the world.

Reverend Keyes is married to a native Filipina, Ethel, and has two children.

For additional information:

- About Reverend Keyes and the MKMI ministry
- About becoming involved in prayer or financial support
- About participating in our annual missions tour
- About obtaining more copies of this book or other books and CD teaching sets

Please contact us at:

- Web: www.mkmi.org
- E-mail: ekeyes@mkmi.org

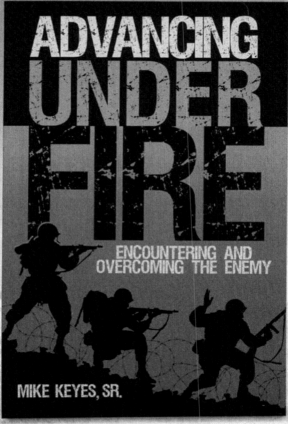

OTHER BOOKS BY
MIKE KEYES SR

Be Strong! Stay Strong!
ISBN: 978-1-939570-00-0

God's perfect will is for every believer to be triumphant and victorious in life. *Be Strong! Stay Strong!* shares seven spiritual priorities and the importance of practicing them consistently, bringing any believer to the place of superior strength and victory over an attack of the enemy in these last days.

Divine Peace
ISBN: 978-1-939570-17-8

How can you live above fear and pressure and the frantic pace of life in these perilous times? *Divine Peace* reveals the principles of knowing and walking in God's peace every day and how to stand strong in the midst of every circumstance with a peace that passes all understanding.

OTHER BOOKS BY
MIKE KEYES SR

Helmet of Hope
ISBN: 978-1-939570-01-7

When a new recruit joins the army, he is issued a helmet and it can mean the difference between life and death in battle. Every spiritual battle is won or lost in the mind - if you lose hope, you've lost your helmet and your head is unprotected. The Helmet of Hope was written to make you a skilled soldier fully prepared for every fight of the faith.

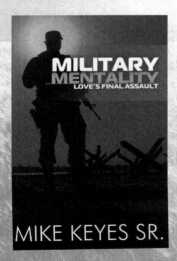

Military Mentality
ISBN: 978-1-936314-98-0

Military Mentality concerns the global war raging at this moment over the souls of humankind. The Body of Christ is at war. Our weapons are different than physical battle and our enemies are not flesh and blood. However, we can apply many crucial lessons learned in wartime to fight our fights of faith today.